The
Columbus
Memoirs
and other tales

First published in the United Kingdom in 2022 by

Mutiny 2000 Publications

www.nicktoczek.com
www.mutiny2000.com

Book layout, typesetting and design by Matt Webster

British Library Cataloguing in Publication Data

A catalogue record for this book is available from the British Library.

ISBN 978-0-9926755-5-4

The Columbus Memoirs

and other tales

*The Lyrics of Nick Toczek & Signia Alpha
and the Story Behind the Albums The Columbus Memoirs,
Walking The Tightrope and Shooting The Messenger*

by

Nick Toczek

and

Matt Webster

mutiny 2000 publications

ACKNOWLEDGEMENTS

Thanks to: Mark Cranmer, Keith Jafrate, Chris Walsh, Jack Atkinson,
Dee Bo General, Emmanuel Williams, Stephen Andrews, Jonny Botterell,
Simon Nolan, Wulf Ingham, Harris and Paul Gray for contributing their
time, energy and talents to our albums
Gaynor Toczek and Britt Jagger for putting up with our bickering and taking photos
Gemma Hobbs of Keighley Creative
Richard Fryer of Penguin Press & Promotion
Liz Austin, who runs the Nick Toczek & Signia Alpha Facebook page
Sean McGhee, editor of RnR magazine
Peter Tomkins of RnR magazine
Rich Deakin of Vive Le Rock!
Nick Burbridge of RnR magazine
Tom Chance of Louder Than War!
Andrew Darlington of International Times
Klemen Breznikar, editor of It's Pschedelic Baby! magazine
Simon Ashberry of BCB Radio
Jane Clayton of West Norfolk Radio
David Pearson of Roots in May
Rick Stuart of Roots & Fusion radio show on
Blues Roots Radio in Canada
Les Ray of Strummers & Dreamers on Cambridge 105 Radio
Dan James of BGfm Radio in Wales
Simon Jones of Anything Goes on Moorlands Radio in Staffordshire
Brian Player of Acoustic Cafe Radio Show on Wey Valley Radio in Hampshire
Michelle Dalgety of Yorkshire Music Collective
David Driver of Writer's Bookshelf on Drystone Radio in Yorkshire
Chris Russell, George & Evie Robinson, Robert Bachman
Maya Jagger, Margery Webster, Crazy Bob
... and everyone who's bought our recordings

Photo credits: Matt Webster - pages 7, 83, 90, 102, 107, 108, 109-114, Tony Woolgar - page 4,
Unknown: page 2, 70, 101 (Matt and Mark), 108 (Emmanuel and Keith), Nick Toczek - page 85,
Simon Nolan - page 105 (older Nogsy), Isabelle Kendall - page 106 (younger Nogsy),
Rowan Robinson - page 110 (older Stephen), Andrea Stevenson - page 104 (Mark), 112 (Harris),
Richard Ingham - page 112 (Nowt), Paul Gray - page 115

All artwork © Matt Webster except *Totally InTOCZEKated* artwork © Nick Toczek

INTRODUCTION

This book is published as a companion piece to *The Columbus Memoirs*, the third vinyl album by Nick Toczek & Signia Alpha, released in June 2022. It follows 2020's debut, *Shooting The Messenger*, and 2021's *Walking The Tightrope*.

In these pages, you'll find the lyrics for all three albums together with extensive notes on the recording of each track plus background information on all those involved.

There's also a CD of *The Columbus Memoirs* which includes five tracks from *Walking The Tightrope* and four from *Shooting The Messenger*.

PART 1: THE LYRICS

WORDSMITH

By Nick Toczek

A part from a few contributions by Matt Webster, all our lyrics are mine. While some of these (notably on this third album) were specifically written for the music, most are drawn from my back-catalogue of poems, stories and lyrics, some recent, others written up to forty years ago. Indeed, an unexpected bonus that's come with this whole collaboration with Signia Alpha has been the chance to revisit and revitalise this past work. I write every day and have done so for decades. I therefore have a vast collection of published and unpublished work to draw on. The chance to explore these personal archives has been both surprising and rewarding.

Why do I write? Partly, it's because this is my chosen job. Mostly, it's to better understand myself. If there's purpose to our lives, which I believe there is, then sharing self-knowledge ranks as second in importance after procreation. Why poetry and short stories? It seems to me that poets and the tellers of concise stories come closest to the necessary truths.

We all need yardsticks. Here is one of mine. Plumbers do plumbing. It's their job. They do it every working day. I have a work ethic. I'm a writer, so I write every day. Here's another. No piece of writing is finished if I haven't learned something from creating it. If I'm no wiser for having written it, then why inflict it on anyone else? And here's one more. A feature of good writing is that you read it and wish that you'd written it. I therefore need to feel exactly that gratitude when reading through something new (or old) that I've written. I have to be both surprised and satisfied by knowing that it's my work.

Born and raised in Bradford, I went to Birmingham University in 1969, began reading and performing my poetry during my three student years, and launched my own poetry magazine, *The Little Word Machine*, in 1972, publishing writers as varied as W.H. Auden, Charles Bukowski, Spike Milligan and Seamus Heaney. The first pamphlet of my own poems, *Because The Evenings*, was also published that year. I'd have fifty further

1

books and pamphlets published over the next half-century. Staying on in Birmingham, in 1974, I co-founded Moseley Community Arts Festival and was its director for several years. Also that year, I founded and ran the poetry and music group, Stereo Graffiti.

For the next three years, we toured throughout the UK, disbanding  in 1977 when I moved back to Bradford, forming the punk rock band Ulterior Motives in the summer of 1978 with my then partner, the singer and guitarist, Kay Russell. Our one 7-inch vinyl single, *Y'Gotta Shout* c/w *Another Lover* came out in 1979, the year that she and I co-founded the seminal indie rock mag, *The Wool City Rocker*, which I continued to edit and publish as a monthly for the next eighteen months. At the end of 1979, Kay and I split up and I met Gaynor. We were married in 1984 and have been together ever since. With an ever-changing line-up, Ulterior Motives continued to gig until it split up in 1982.

From March 1982 until April 1986, I ran a wide variety of weekly punk and indie rock gigs at numerous venues throughout the Leeds-Bradford area, sometimes running as many as five events per week. I'm writing a history of these which will eventually be published in book-form. Meanwhile, you can find it as a work-in-progress on my website.

In September 1986, I formed a business partnership with fellow Bradford poet, Wild Willi Beckett, who was also the frontman of The Psycho Surgeons and Shadow Minister of Mental Health for The Monster Raving Loony Party. Together, we set up a regular weekly alternative cabaret club, one of the first in northern England. Our mix of comedians, solo musicians, poets, circus acts, bands and a host of truly eccentric performers proved a success and continued for more than five years. Among the comedians to whom we gave gigs early in their careers were Jo Brand, Jack Dee, Lucy Porter, Steve Coogan, Dave Gorman, Linda Smith, Peter

Kay, Ross Noble, Julian Clary, Jimeoin, Jo Caulfield, Tony Burgess, Hovis Presley, Jenny Le Coat, Simon Fanshawe, Henry Normal, Jeremy Hardy, John Dowie and Tony Allen. Alternative cabaret was a truly exciting, innovative, provocative and constantly evolving arena during the late 1980s and early 1990s. Willi and I had an extraordinary time working together. We got to use some sadly long-gone but truly memorable Bradford venues such as Nick Treadwell's wonderful art gallery and ancient pubs like The Royal Standard and The Spotted House. It's also worth mentioning that each of our events was linked with a particular charity or worthy cause. Every week, we'd raise money, distribute info and publicity, and often feature a speaker from the featured organisa- tion. We did this because Willi and I both felt that mere entertainment, without any humanitarian or social responsibility, simply cushioned crap government. We wanted to kick against that.

Matt Webster and I have known one another since the early 1980s. However, it wasn't until late on in 2006 that we first began working together. I had some unreleased studio recordings of the seminal Brad- ford punk band The Negativz. Matt had copies of rare live recordings. We'd both been friends and fans of the band. Singer, Dave Wilcox, had sadly died of a heroin overdose and we wanted to document their bril- liance. The outcome was the 26-track CD album, *Mental Case*, which came out on Matt's Mutiny 2000 label in March 2007.

The premature death from cancer, that same month, of Wild Willi Beckett, brought Matt and me together again when, with other friends of Willi, we brought out and promoted his posthumous single, *Kingdom Come, Bring It On!*. The b-side was Willi's first ever song, *Straw Hats,* on which he was backed by the original line-up of the band New Model Army. Released by Mutiny 2000 Records on what would have been his sixtieth birthday, it was - in accordance with his dying wishes - pressed in fluorescent green vinyl in which his ashes had been scattered. You can see these multi-coloured fragments of him glinting in each copy of the disc. Hardly a day goes by, even now, when I don't remember and miss the man. He was a much loved and popular Bradford character. That's probably why, when we were planning the release of the single, his other friends rejected as 'too sick' my suggestion that we promote the disc containing bits of him with a slogan which I still reckon he'd have loved: 'Have a little Willi'.

Ever since then, Matt and I have regularly collaborated. The first of what would become a plethora of projects was also in 2007. During the

3

1980s Bluurg Records had released five albums of my work. Four were on cassette. The fifth, released in 1987, was an 11-track vinyl album, *InTOCZEKated*. Bluurg was the label owned and run by Dick Lucas, front-man of The Subhumans, Culture Shock and more recently Citizen Fish and Bus Station Loonies. The cassette albums were primarily of perfor-mance poetry, but the vinyl album was of my work with various bands. In 2007, twenty years on from that release, I'd recorded many more songs, some of which had been on compilation albums, while others were unreleased. Releasing a much extended version of that Bluurg album seemed like a great way to bring all these recordings together. The result was my 25-track CD album, *Totally InTOCZEKated*, which

Matt released on Mutiny 2000 Records towards the end of 2007. I love this album. Span-ning the decade from 1977 to 1987, it contains a really diverse range of songs on which I work with some great musicians. There's Wreckless Eric, skin-head band The Burial, US punks Toxic Reasons (guesting Derek Greening from Peter & The Test Tube Babies and the late Mick

Crudge from The Fits), two-tone & reggae band Spectre, To Be Contin-ued (who soon after morphed into The Dead Vaynes, later The Vaynes), the wonderfully eccentric post-Hippie combo Apocalypse Choir, lovable punx Dan, plus various incarnations of my own band Ulterior Motives… and even a taster of my previous group, Stereo Graffiti.

As Matt explains later in this book, his debilitating ailments then took him out of active involvement in music for almost a decade. During this time he and Gary Cavanagh worked on *Bradford's Noise Of The Valleys*, their ongoing comprehensive history, via a series books and CDs, of Bradford-related music since the 1960s. They first contacted me because they wanted to include my activities in their first book and use one of my recordings on one of their CDs. Highly impressed with what they were doing, I went on to write a series of reviews and articles about these CDs and books and the project as a whole. Most of these were published in the bi-monthly UK music mag, *RnR* (formerly *R2* and, before that, *Rock'n'Reel*), for which I've been a regular columnist, features-writer and reviewer since 2008. I also regularly played tracks from these CDs on the weekly one-hour FM radio show which I presented for twenty years (1991-2021) on BCB Radio (Bradford Community Broadcasting).

In 2018, as Matt began to emerge from the decade-long lockdown which his ill-health had imposed on him, he and I were able to resume our active collaborations. Back in 2012, I'd had some short-run CD releases via Bradford-based label, Sound Shack. Among these was *Motormouth*, a 3-CD set of 46 performance poems. Matt helped me to repackage these tracks as a 2-CD release through my own Not-A-Roity label. Later that same year, Matt's Mutiny 2000 label followed this with a brand new 2-CD spoken-word release, *Dealing With The Darkness*, which featured 49 of my more serious poems. It was in early 2019, after he'd worked on these albums, that Matt first suggested our musical collaboration as Nick Toczek & Signia Alpha.

Prior to that, Matt had persuaded me that what I now needed was an all-singing, all-dancing website to promote me, my work and my many books and recordings. He and his partner, Britt Jagger, were designing websites. He showed me some of these. They looked great. I was more than impressed and knew that he could and would deliver the goods. Check it out. My ever-extending website (www.nicktoczek.com) testifies to this.

Nick Toczek & Signia Alpha got underway early in 2019. Matt had grand plans, and I was totally up for working with him once again. Those projects on which we'd first co-operated back in 2007 had left me deeply impressed by Matt's diversity of skills and his unflinching commitment to every task. All I'd seen of him and his work since then had only bolstered my faith in him. His battling drive and sure-footed seriousness of purpose persuaded me that here was someone with a work ethic which was more than a match for mine.

Matt chose the perfect time to suggest our collaboration. I was already working successfully with two other music men, the classical composer Malcolm Singer and the German punk-rocker, song-writer and multi-instrumentalist Thies Marsen. I worked distantly with both of these. What Matt offered was, from the outset, a very different prospect. He lived less than a mile from my home, with a great studio in his front room plus a huge rehearsal space and studio just five miles away in a Bradford mill. We could work closely.

Living in London, Malcolm Singer was Director of Music at the Yehudi Menuhin School and a professor of Composition at the Guildhall School of Music and Drama. We'd begun collaborating in 1997. Our *Dragons Cantata* (using my dragon poems set to his music) premiered at London's Royal Albert Hall in 1998. We then turned the work into a full musical which was published as *Dragons! The Musical* by Golden Apple in 2005. Meanwhile, our second cantata, *Perfect Pitch* (using my football poems and his music), premiered at The Barbican in London. Both premieres feature combined school choirs of hundreds of children plus a full orchestra. Then, in 2010, Malcolm and I completed our first full opera, *The Jailer's Tale*. This was a political story which I'd based on Guantanamo Bay. It premiered that year at London's Arts Depot. Now, in 2022, Malcolm and I are, once more, collaborating on an update of *Perfect Pitch* which is due to have several performances towards the end of the year. We're also discussing possible future collaborations.

My work with Thies Marsen, who lives in Bavaria, came about by chance. I'd had a poem, *Noo Yawk Chant / Sheer Funk*, used as the opening track on a compilation album, *God Save Us From The USA*, which had been released in 1987 in support of the Nicaragua Solidarity Campaign. Years later, Thies (pronounced Teas) bought a copy of this album and, in 2001, chopped up my words and set them to his music. In 2010, after chancing on a website which gave my email address, he sent me the track. An email exchange ensued which resulted in him taking more of my recorded poems and setting these to music.

In 2012, I played these tracks to a local musician friend, Nagbea, who ran the record label Sound Shack. He really liked them and, later that year, Sound Shack released our debut 3-track CD, *The Bavariations EP*. Because we'd communicated by email, Thies and I now had our first recordings available without having ever met or even spoken to one another. In 2013, however, a German radio station heard about our long-distance collaboration and commissioned him to make a radio documentary about us. He phoned me. We spoke for the first time. He came to Bradford for a couple of days. We met up and made the recordings for him to edit into that documentary. That's the only time we've ever met. While he was in Bradford, I'd given him a copy of the Sound Shack edition of *Motormouth*. This enabled him to work on putting more of my recorded poems to music.

We both had busy lives, so it wasn't until 2016 that he emailed me another finished track. Four more followed in the last three months of 2018. Could we do an album? More tracks followed in quick succession. By February 2019, we'd twelve tracks which we agreed would be the

6

album. During March, Matt and I put the album together and I released it as *The Bavariations Album* in CD format on my Not-A-Rioty label. Other tracks followed via email, resulting, in January 2021, in a second Nick Toczek & Thies Marsen album. Pressed in blood-red vinyl, this was *Death & Other Destinations*, the first 12-inch disc released on Not-A-Rioty. Thies has since finished more tracks and we've now got enough material for a third album which may well come out on CD from Not-A-Rioty towards the end of 2021.

Working with Matt has been a fast-moving, diverse and prolific process which has already resulted in two lengthy CD albums, a dozen download-only singles and three beautifully packaged coloured vinyl

albums, all within less than three years.

Work on what became our first album, *Shooting The Messenger*, began in 2019. The finished product made two very different appearances. In January 2020 we released it as a 17-track CD. Ten months later, in November 2020, came the remixed and much edited version, a 12-track disc on purple vinyl which became the definitive recording. Our second album, *Walking The Tightrope*, was released on transparent yellow vinyl in March 2021. The third album, *The Columbus Memoirs*, pressed in blue and white marbled vinyl and released in June 2022 is our rockiest album yet. As with our first album, the vinyl version of this new album was preceded by a longer CD. Released in February 2022 and also called *The Columbus Memoirs*, it consisted of all ten album tracks plus five sample tracks from *Walking The Tightrope* and four from *Shooting The Messenger*.

Matt played many of the instruments on all three albums and I did most of the vocals, but we also had a dozen excellent guest contributors. All of these were Matt's musical associates with the single exception of Dee Bo General who was a long-time friend of mine.

So here we are, with our third album completed and a fourth already under discussion. Bring it on!

The Columbus Memoirs

THE COLUMBUS MEMOIRS

SIDE 1

1. THE HOUR GLASS (4.13) (Toczek/Webster)
2. ANOTHER SHORELINE (4.03) (Toczek/Webster)
3. TIME TRIPPER (4.58) (Toczek/Webster)
4. THREADS (3.21) (Toczek/Webster)
5. DEAD LINES (2.36) (Toczek/Webster)
6. JUST FOR A MOMENT (2.05) (Webster)

SIDE 2

1. MOONWATCHERS (3.47) (Toczek/Webster)
2. FOUR AND A HALF (3.46) (Toczek/Webster/Atkinson)
3. THE COLUMBUS MEMOIRS (7.22) (Toczek/Cranmer/Jafrate/Webster)
4. DIGNITY (4.48) (Toczek/Webster/Ingham)

THE HOUR GLASS

(words: Nick Toczek & Matt Webster / music: Matt Webster)

Time is the movie in which we play minor roles.
Time ticks and time tricks us with the illusion of eternity.
Time waits like a wolf at the door.

Time flows from us like water, blows through us like a breeze.
Time takes a silhouette and puts it in your mind.
Time takes a sweet regret
And leaves it somewhere you can't find.
Time never sleeps, but always dreams.
Time is a lifelong joke with a killer punchline.

Have you got enough time?

Time ticks another tock
And makes a new tomorrow
Till the clock slips another cog
And the time you're on is borrowed.

Time takes the witnesses who shared your story.
Time is now.
We ride it out of the past and into the future.
Time grinds diamonds into sand
And that sand fills another hourglass.
Time is a roulette wheel on which we bet until we're broke.

Have you got enough time?

Time ticks another tock
And makes a new tomorrow
Till the clock slips another cog
And the time you're on is borrowed.

Time drips another drop.
The seconds seem to linger
As the sand from the hour glass
Is running through your fingers.

Time is neither linear nor real.
Time is the God without whom nothing exists.
Time is what everything takes
But in the end, time takes everything.

Time turns new with second hand.
Time despises the constant grovelling of clocks.

Time ticks another tock
And makes a new tomorrow
Till the clock slips another cog
And the time you're on is borrowed.

Time drips another drop.
The second seems to linger
As the sand from the hour glass
Is running through your fingers.

NICK: *After I'd written several lyrics on the time theme, none of which he'd felt fitted, Matt suggested that we each write a series of one-line abstract / surreal definitions of time. Co-writing the album's first lyric seemed to me like a great way to show that our work was a wholly collaborative venture and not, as some past reviewers had appeared to think, me working with backing musicians. This is our first lyrical collaboration.*

MATT: *I'd always heard this as a TV theme tune for a remake of The Time Tunnel or some such fantastical time travel adventure. I was also thinking of the way music (or a photo or even a smell) can transport you in time, almost literally. For a moment, you're back in that place where you heard a certain song. You experience an emotional burst that fades as soon as you try to analyse it. Such is the mystery of our conception of time and the effect that the passing of it has upon our minds. Is the glass of hours half full or half empty?*

11

ANOTHER SHORELINE

(words: Nick Toczek / music: Matt Webster)

Now the shoreline lies before us
As our ship's bow ploughs into port
To a new land where new life
Fills the bewildered milling quayside
Where staring strangers are gathered there to greet us.

Fate saved our souls as we braved
Roaring gales and sea-monsters' jaws
Which all strove to swallow us whole
But now lie lost in our wake
Across the aching ocean acres guilty of taking us,
Kidnapped, press-ganged, forever from our homes.

And so her shoreline hauls us all in
Like some fresh catch of netted fish.
And we will soon forget our former homes,
Lost histories, stolen loves and lives.
But we will build ourselves a better time
Beneath this discovered canopy of alien stars
And anchor ourselves firmly in this new found land.

CHORUS *(Matt Webster)*

A new dawn, another shoreline.
A new dawn, another shoreline.
A new dawn, another shoreline.
A new dawn, another shoreline.

NICK: *The first song recorded for this album was 'The Columbus Memoirs'. Coming out of the global paralysis of the Covid pandemic, we decided this LP should have travel as its central theme. 'The Hour Glass' deals with time, which governs all journeys. Another Shoreline is about the arrival of 'settlers', the euphemism white western immigrants and refugees used for themselves when they invaded and took over a country.*

TIME TRIPPER

(words: Nick Toczek / music: Matt Webster)

We'll begin well beyond the late-Victorian imaginings of H.G. Wells. Come with me, pressing forward half-a-century plus.

We're in the 1950s, gone from England to America. We're with the CIA, conducting covert mind control experiments. Here's where we first feel ourselves slightly slipping on time's tenuous banana skin. And we see objects instantly shift locations. An inkling you'd have missed if you'd blinked.

Lose ten more years. Somewhere in the 1960s, we'll almost touch time-travel again, oh so nearly peeling ourselves away from the now, almost actually letting go to tumble into the future-past on a whole host of hallucinogens - peyote, LSD, magic mushrooms and more.

Oh, but then we lost it. Lost the plot, simply got swallowed. Stole ourselves a century of shallow selfishness. We'll jump that hurdle too.

And here we are. At the true start of our journey. We're on a warming planet where nothing that's nailed here will survive. This will be our most ambitious leap, one millennium forward, so that we can survive, and life goes on.

Wish us luck.

NICK: *Taking its name from The Beatles song 'Day Tripper', this is a fantastic / fanciful account of time travel from the 19th century onwards.*

THREADS

(words: Nick Toczek / music: Matt Webster)

New day. You wake. Earthquaked. Body bound in bedsheets. Head held entirely trapped under its debris of collapsing dreams.

Straightened out, you hit the streets. Thickly tangled trails of traffic track and trace the entire tapestries of countless lives. This close-packed global mesh seethes, ceaselessly.

Deep in the dense, dark, undead earth beneath, packed trains shuttle down tunnels, gas and water pump through pipelines, cables carry currents.

Overhead, planes pace planetary pathways and, threading through the brains of the living, billions of thoughts per second commute.

Stretched between uncounted catacombs of rooms, taut wires team with voices and images, as does the entire ether via higher satellites.

Yet, see you, woven well within your secrecy of walls and windows, believing yourself mercifully deaf to the sin of such a cacophonous din.

NICK: *Journeys are ubiquitous. They're there in our dreams. They're in the flow of traffic on our roads and electricity down power lines. They're there in flightpaths, brainwaves, phonecalls, emails, and other internet messaging. These and more weave a complex mesh which wraps and entraps us.*

DEAD LINES

(words: Nick Toczek / music: Matt Webster)

It's September in New York City. Days shorten and their balmy evenings populate piano-bars with jaded journalists, wordsmiths of world-weary wisdom, authors of an uncertain age who're handsomely paid to pit their pithy wits by penning pieces impaling the mood of the moment, zooming in on the zeitgeist.

The barmen are there to pour them all one more. one more and one more for the road. But theirs is never a novel, only an endless stream of counted column inches which map the monthlies, weeklies and dailies of this city's magazine-stands.

It's the late 1940s. What drives their writing is a blend of alcohol and chain-smoking. With a war just won, their thoughts tumble as freely as autumn's falling leaves, and cynicism rules.

Dorothy Parker, Lillian Helman, Martha Gellhorn, Hedda Hopper, Walter Lippmann, H.L Mencken, Louella Parsons, Dorothy Thompson, Walter Winchell.

NICK: *Matt's music evoked a late-night New York jazz bar. Once again, I wrote several pieces which didn't quite work, before going back in time and crossing the Atlantic with this tale of 1940s American newspaper columnists, nine of whom I list in my subliminally whispered second vocal.*

JUST FOR A MOMENT

(words & music: Matt Webster)

Just for a moment
I thought I saw you.
Just for a moment
I thought heard your voice.

I remembered all the times that you were there.
That summer, that day, that year.

But you were never in this room.
You were never in this house,
In his street.

But, just for a moment,
I thought you were still alive.
I thought you were still alive.

NICK: *To further prove that Signia Alpha is a fully active entity in this collaboration, here's a track, travelling back in memory, in which I play no part whatsoever.*

MATT: *I'm sure we've all had that moment where you catch a glimpse of someone or hear a voice you think you recognise. There's an instant before memory and realisation kicks in and you remember that the person you thought was there is no longer with us. The deeper the love, the harder that little moment hurts.*

MOONWATCHERS

(words: Nick Toczek / music: Matt Webster)

I was there…

was there when this moon secured control of tides and seas
then demanded bats and owls and more night beasts like these.

I was there…

witnessed when she climbed the sky and fell back down again,
watched the way, while she was full, torn minds would turn insane.

I was there…

as a child, watching moonbeams dance on slumber's cover,
saw her dreamy light unite loner with a lover.

I was there…

when my moon and midnight met and celebrated mass,
knew her hue of deepest blue could never come to pass.

And I am here…

man in moon, see him shine, feel him stretch my face and spine,
man in me made lupine, grey fur coats this form of mine.

where spectral moonlight conjures its ghosts and ghouls from graves,
and vampire gangs craving blood comb city streets in waves.

CHORUS *(Matt Webster)*

Embrace the darkness. Welcome the night,
Drink my health with absinthe in the moonlight.
Toast your soul with absinthe in the moonlight.

NICK: *Literally and metaphorically, the moon has always exerted its unique pull on us. I wrote this in 2020 for an anthology of moon poems. While all my lyrics on side one were written specifically for this album, the four on side two were pre-existing pieces.*

MATT: *I thought the moon theme worked well with the Gothic feel of the music although I felt it needed a twist. I asked Nick to add the 'reveal' about the watcher being a werewolf and added a chorus lyric.*

FOUR AND A HALF

(words: Nick Toczek / music: Matt Webster & Jack Atkinson)

A bare room in the bus depot and I sit on a bench. Standing in front of me is a bored teenager. No more than seventeen, he wears a military uniform. He's playing a game with no words. Listening carefully to music on his iPod, he casually waves a loaded rifle round the room. Pointing it first at a wall, then straight into my face, then out of the window, targeting a succession of passers by.

When I was his age and drunk on holiday in Italy, me and some local lads got into an argument with the police. It grew heated, one of the lads hit a young cop. We all ran away, laughing.

Suddenly, bullets from an automatic began thudding into the wall above our heads. I dived through a doorway. A whole family, sitting around their dinner table, mid meal, glanced up to see me, a mad Englishman, sauntering drunkenly past them through their kitchen and away.

Years later, touring America with a couple of punk bands, a cop stopped us after midnight on a beach somewhere in Los Angeles. He told us to take our hands out of our pockets. When I didn't, he pulled out a gun and stuck it against my head.

I got angry, or is arrogant a better word? Anyway, I refused, saying, "I'm English and I'm not used to cops with guns. Ask me nicely!" "Take your f###ing hands out of your f###ing pockets now!" he said.

Motionless, I stared back at him... "Just do it, Nick," said my friends. So I shrugged and held up my hands. Turning to the others, the cop told them, "I didn't know if he had a gun, I wasn't gonna wait and see. "

Then, addressing me, he added, "You're lucky, I was counting to five before pulling the trigger, I'd got to four and a half..."

> **NICK:** *As a writer in schools and also as a performer-poet for older audiences, I've visited dozens of countries, in the course of which I've had guns pulled on me many times. The bus depot was in Indonesia.*

THE COLUMBUS MEMOIRS

(words: Nick Toczek / music: Mark Cranmer, Keith Jafrate & Matt Webster)

Yesterday, I came across America while clearing out the cupboard in the back room. Picked it up. Opened it at New York. Streets that hadn't been dusted in years. Took out a skyscraper and lit it, towering inferno that tasted fine. Decided to write the book...

It was late spring. That morning I went to the garden and dug up the biplane. Wings that glinted in the sun, it flew better than ever before And I determined, there and then, to take up that option on the necessary airspace to mount a voyage of discovery.

So we systematically killed off their buffalo herds. Nowadays we'd destroy their factories, same difference.

Came in low over Manhattan. Monday: built The White House. Tuesday: erected The Statue of Liberty. Refuelling in a small town in the West of Ireland, "America?" repeated the man as he passed me the last of the cans of gasoline. Sunday: played baseball and built a church. Custer's death on the evening news.

Arrival is immunisation, immigration, passport control and The Committee of Unamerican Activities. Departure was: cancel milk and papers, leave front-door key with the neighbour, switch off gas and electricity. Reports high cloud and clear weather ahead, little sign of air turbulence. The wings glinted. Three week supply of food and drink.

Landed in New Hampshire. Climbed down from the cockpit. A small step for man but...

Designed a flag. Built a cabin. Learned my zip code number off by heart. Watched our civil war from the roof of The Empire State Building.

Got home in time to catch the Late Late Show. Or else, I rang some friends... party, my place. And we talked things over, decided to call them 'dollars'.

Later, we go out, buy hamburgers. The guy, he likes our money, we like his burgers.

At the drive-in movie, she suggested 'colour' could be changed to 'color' without a 'u'. On the way home, I said, "... and 'thru' instead of 'through', OK?" She said it sounded fine to her, so we got married, had two kids, and decided to head west in search of gold and a new life.

Thirteen stars, that was obvious, but how many stripes? Later, we added more stars and bought Alaska, wholesale.

Put an ad in The New York Times. It read: 'Wanted, covered wagon, two horses, will exchange for biplane – good flyer, only one previous owner.'

A hundred miles out we join up with a wagon train. It features John Wayne, RIP, and we each get twelve dollars a day as extras, union rates in those days.

And the kids died, one of fever before we'd reached the Midwest, the other in Korea.

Some work in Hollywood before the depression. Made some dealing in slavery. Lost it all in a poker game.

Marriage annulled. Hoboed, swept bars, bummed cigarettes and stole. Got drunk more times than I could count. Threw crates of tea into the harbour. Those were the days!

I could dance as well as Fred Astaire in my youth. Do you remember Sly & the Family Stone at Woodstock? Far out! Do you remember the Alamo? Too much! Do you remember who cut down the cherry tree and never told a lie? Groovy, baby!

Watergate? And the way the wings glinted in the sun. Do you remember all of that?

I won a Purple Heart in Vietnam, killed children and mainlined, swore allegiance and swore, and still hate Puerto Ricans. Ecology, cosmology, Walt Whitman's white beard, and the collective guilt. I was with Lincoln when he okayed the dropping of the H Bomb on Cuba. We drove out the British, imported apples and horses and God. Marketed tobacco and coffee and black musicians.

I rode pillion with Pancho Villa on a Harley Davidson 74 paid for by the CIA. By day, we dealt in drugs and guns. By night, bugged and burgled by Presidents, we slept beneath the Star Wars, dreaming of our Nazi past, to wake up one day beside James Dean, were with him still when he died of AIDS.

And we were waiting on the quayside whenever they shipped in the zipped-up, handsome, homecoming hero stiffs, were cheering when they lowered the last of the batch into oceans of empty rhetoric. We buried Buddy Holly in a jukebox.

My motto was: 'the only good Injun's a dead one'. We used to sing all the time: a penny whistle, a banjo, a guitar, a drum. Proud songs that made tall men.

I remember it all as if it were yesterday: "Yes," I said to him, "America!" and climbed up into the cockpit. The wings just glinted.

NICK: *Back in the 1980s, having read an interesting article on the cut-up technique of writing which was pioneered by Dadaists in the 1920s and subsequently used successfully by both William Burroughs and David Bowie, I thought I'd have a go. It seemed to fit well with my somewhat fragmentary knowledge of American history.*

DIGNITY

(words: Nick Toczek / music: Matt Webster & Wulf Ingham)

Dignity…

For those on the run
From the prison, the gun;
For those who escape
After torture and rape;
For those who are homeless and hopeless and stateless;
For those grown so thin, they could almost be weightless;

For those left too weak
Or too frightened to speak,
Like the poor kid who hid
But who saw what they did;

For those who've not eaten,
The pursued and the beaten
Who fled when the harvest had failed,
Who came home to loved ones impaled;
For those who've walked and walked and walked from far away
to here;
For the traveller who doesn't need a bloody souvenir;

For those who wake up from their dreams
Shaken by shadows and screams;
For those who were lucky to lose just a limb;
For those from the boat who were able to swim;

Yes, dignity,
If you please…

For those not given the chance to choose
Who carry the little they've got left to lose;
For those who've been moved on so often before
That they don't even care where they are any more;

For those for whom water is worth more than gold;
For those who've held children whose bodies turned cold;

For those who now know that they'll never return;
For those who've watched all that life meant to them burn…

Just give me some dignity.
Just give me some dignity.

NICK: *Worldwide, refugees and migrants are demonised and systematically mistreated. The wealthiest nations are the most guilty in this respect, with Britain and America shamefully leading the field. I'm therefore particularly pleased to have this poem / lyric included here. Obviously it chimes, chillingly, with the album's twinned themes of travel and the passage of time.*

MATT: *Very powerful and relevant lyrics matched with a powerful driving backing led to us choosing this for the first single from the album.*

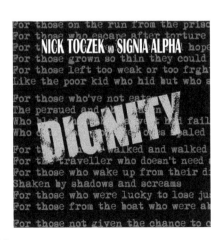

23

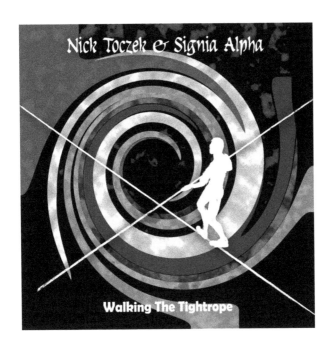

WALKING THE TIGHTROPE

SIDE 1

1. THE MOVIE (3.09) (Toczek/Webster)
2. BEST WISHES (5.49) (Toczek/Webster/Ingham)
3. CONFIDENCE TRICK (3.55) (Toczek/Webster)
4. MOON ABOVE THE MÖVENPICK (3.03) (Toczek/Webster)
5. ALGEBRA (3.07) (Toczek/Webster/Atkinson)
6. THE DETECTIVE (1.00) (Webster)

SIDE 2

1. CANNIBALS OF THE WESTERN WORLD (4.06) (Toczek/Webster)
2. NOTHING RESOLVES (5.15) (Toczek/Webster/Cranmer)
3. HOTEL MUSIC (3.14) (Toczek/Webster)
4. GALLEON (3.29) (Toczek/Webster/Atkinson)
5. CLOSE UP (4.54) (Toczek/Cranmer/Webster)

THE MOVIE

(words: Nick Toczek / music: Matt Webster)

Driving the car.
Touching the gun.
Finding the street.
You write the book and I'll script the movie.

The eternal victim of the cowboy hero terrorist popstar walks habitually into bullets and they tunnel through him.

All day long, he tumbles dramatically onto pavements, clutching his chest.

You write the book and I'll script the movie.

He draws the crowds like a white-face circus clown in a red shirt.

'Roll up! Roll up for the real thing!'

There's nothing braver than death, except its infliction.

And the we-did-it phone call is a fine trick to pull off at the end of a perfect performance.

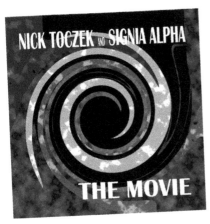

NICK: *I've always wanted to make movies. I once played a minor acting role in a low-budget independent film. On another occasion, I was an actor in a TV advert but my scene was cut from the final version. Back in the mid-1970s, I'd an unpublished novel which was being made into a film. However, when the couple playing the twin lead split up acrimoniously, the whole project had to be abandoned. This lyric fits within that same framework. It's just another episode in my unfulfilled film career.*

BEST WISHES

(words: Nick Toczek / music: Matt Webster & Wulf Ingham)

I wish you far from danger and despair,
And further still from those who just don't care.
I wish you shorter hours, better pay.
I wish you luck in all you do and say.

I wish the telephone would one day ring
And bring a voice not selling anything.
I wish you brass in pocket, food on plate
And time at end of day to contemplate.

Some days I wish your "No" had been a "Yes"
And often wish for more, and then for less.
I wish we occupied a better place
In which war gleaned not glory but disgrace.

I wish you jobs well done and comfy shoes
With music and whatever else you choose,
And kindnesses and moments which amaze
To cruise you down the distance of your days.

I wish you high ambition all your life
And strength when guilt cuts deep as any knife.
I wish you distant journeys and returns
And wish you passion so intense it burns.

I sometimes wish I liked myself much more
And we could cure what makes us insecure.
I wish us doors which don't require keys
And wish us never forced down on our knees.

However, I'd be satisfied with this:
Us dazzled by one glimpse of gleaming bliss.

NICK: *Wishes fill the yawning gap between what we hope for and what we actually achieve. Make what you like of these ones - some address to me, some to you.*

CONFIDENCE TRICK

(words: Nick Toczek / music: Matt Webster)

What if I loved you less
Could kill this intensity
Would never need to ask again if anything was wrong
And were not your impossible lover
Nor you mine?

And what if there was the money here
For me to treat us as I would?

You see, I have inside me
This better version of myself,
This never jealous man
Who is always going to one day turn up at your door.

His clothes are new.
He has come to take you
On some grand and endless adventure.

NICK: *An equally vast space opens up between intentions and outcomes. So here's a lyric about that frustration.*

MOON ABOVE THE MÖVENPICK

(words: Nick Toczek / music: Matt Webster)

Another night and the air lies thick.
The moon sits over The Mövenpick.
Idle drivers chat. Low planes growl through.

Ending their shift, a construction crew
Waits for their lift in the dust and heat
Where they stand or squat or slump dead-beat.

Amid bits of brickwork, concrete, tar,
A loud kitten crouched beneath a car
Innocently makes us all aware

Of Earthly sin. Then the call to prayer
Sees faith and fear intertwine details,
Muezzin's voice mixed with feline wails.

God-of-all-things, you've got much to do:
Weather, work, wildlife, wickedness too.
This night needs you and the air lies thick.

The moon sits over The Mövenpick.

NICK: *I've been a visiting writer in schools in Doha on several occasions. This was written during my first visit. The city was fast-expanding and much of it consisted of building sites. I was staying in The Gloria, but eating most nights in the bar of the nearby Mövenpick. This is about my route between the two hotels.*

ALGEBRA

(words: Nick Toczek / music: Matt Webster & Jack Atkinson)

The exasperating imprecision of language.
Keep a grip.
Aimless after midnight.
Wandering from room to room in a house I can't afford
Doubting my vision.

There was snowfall and love in the evening.
I counted forty-one political killings on today's news.

Too tired to argue, I retreat into my own existence,
Almost convinced that it's not what you believe,
But that you believe.

So passions are paramount.
Enter jealousy and the fear of loss.
You can't get round the fact that unacceptable equations
Occupy the ringside seats.

Aim lower.
Watch a soap opera.
Play a game.
Tell a joke.
Cop out.
Do anything.

I attach too much importance to the words.

NICK: *Being a full-time professional writer becomes an obsessive pursuit in which everything tends to be perceived as mere writing-fodder. This can cut you off from the day-to-day flow of human life, as is happening in this lyric.*

THE DETECTIVE

(words & music: Matt Webster)

It wasn't a dark night,
It wasn't even raining,
but the phone rang anyway.

'I found the answer,' said the voice. 'It was here all along.'

'What did you find?', I asked her.

'You tell me,' she replied, 'You're the detective."

MATT: *I wrote the music as a 1960s detective theme. I'd imagined a voice-over by Humphry Bogart, 'It was a dark and stormy night...'*

NICK: *Matt had a clear idea of what he wanted wordwise to accompany his music. I made several attempts to write something suitable, but none matched what he'd envisaged, so I suggested he write the words. This short piece is therefore the first recording I've ever made in which I perform words I've not written.*

CANNIBALS OF THE WESTERN WORLD

(words: Nick Toczek / music: Matt Webster)

Like soft fruit we're boxed up.
We're banged up and lidded.
We're stacked away, packed away,
Pre-taxed and gridded;

Apartmented, motorised,
Mortgaged and kiddied;
Each income computed
And suitably quidded.

Then citified, pitiful,
Puddled and giddied,
We're herded on waggons
And wheelied and skidded.

We're animals, we're the common herd.
We're the cannibals of the western world.
We're animals, we're the common herd.
We're the cannibals of the western world.
Cannibals of the western world...

We're bundled to market
And monied and bidded
And cutted and gutted
And bloodied and ridded
And sliced up and eaten
And each of us did it.

We're animals, we're the common herd.
We're cannibals of the western world.
We're animals, we're the common herd.
We're cannibals of the western world.
Cannibals of the western world...
Cannibals of the western world.

CANNIBALS RAP

(Nick Toczek)

We're those feeding. We're their food.
Hear us chomping. We're the chewed.
We're the diners. Eat us, dude.

We're the starving. We're the stewed.
Farmed and fattened, caged and zooed.
Roasted, toasted, boiled, baked, brewed.

We're the flesh that's much valued.
Hunters hunted. Prey pursued.
We're the mincemeat. We're menu'd.

We're the mass, the multitude.
We're the flock, the breed, the brood.
We're here to be barbecued.

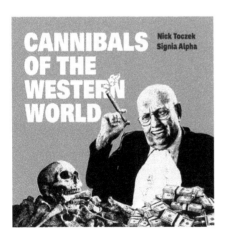

NICK: *Thriving in a world of mass poverty, we wealthy westerners are the real cannibals, luxuriating in all that we refuse to share with the needy and disadvantaged. I already had the main lyric, but wrote 'Cannibals Rap' specially for Dee Bo General to perform.*

NOTHING RESOLVES

(words: Nick Toczek / music: Matt Webster & Mark Cranmer)

You live on the edge of a knife.
Nothing resolves.
Whatever you touch is sand.
It drains from you
Until you can't put a price on anything.
You feel like a supermarket that's afraid to open.
But glass breaks.
Shapes change.
Nothing waits for you.
Nothing waits.

People are deserting language in their hundreds.
You might as well speak Latin.
You might as well write Greek.
You're a joke who put his punchline in his pocket...
But couldn't find it when the time came.
And then the time came, and came again, and again
Like a bad dream, like a passion.
It's only fashion.
Like a passion.
It's only fashion.

You're gonna pull though,
Fix it, find success and true happiness:
The right brand of cigarette to start you smoking again,
The right brand of drink to make you daily drunk,
The right blend of compromises to make you famous...
But each day rips its own pages from the book.

You stand in a windy street waiting for a bus.
It's the wrong stop, the wrong fare in your hand,
The wrong time of day.

You decide to walk, knowing it's too far.
The right bus pulls up just after you've gone.
The right money was in your pocket all the time.
You're walking nowhere, into a mirror.
Always face-to-face with yourself,
You live on the edge of a knife.

Nothing resolves.
Nothing resolves.

RAP *(Dee Bo General)*

I'm just a poet man, always alive.
I'm just a poet man, always survive.
With feelings, meaning and notions.
The usual poem put in motion.

NICK: *The most rewarding aspect of being a writer by profession is that you get to make your living through what would otherwise be a hobby. In other words, you're doing a job you love. The downside is that, to keep going, you need to have absolute faith in yourself and what you're doing. There are times when that's far from easy.*

GALLEON

(words: Nick Toczek / music: Matt Webster & Jack Atkinson)

The ghost ship glides through coastal fog.
A ghastly hand scrawls in the log:
Have pity on us, please.

High scraps of sail hang torn to shreds
And rigging rots, the ropes in threads
On flat and windless seas.

And wet weeds clamber up the wreck,
And crabs crawl cruel across the deck,
Legs bent like broken knees.

The air is bad, the silence worse,
No shanty sung nor sailor's curse
Since thirst and since disease.

Skeleton crew, it's truly that,
The bare-boned captain, men and cat
Might shake like rattled keys.

But treasure glitters in the hold,
And greed goes gladly after gold
To trap men by degrees.

So, hooked by hoard and its reward,
The ship finds more to lure aboard
Like mice pursuing cheese.

But once they're there, they have to stay.
With no way off, they waste away
Or in the cold fog freeze.

Thus this galleon slowly goes
On one vast voyage no human chaos
And years pass like a breeze.

NICK: *Many of the poems I've written for children work just as well for an adult audience. Here's an example. It's one of a few dozen scary poems in an as-yet-unpublished children's collection of mine which draws heavily on my love of horror films. Life's busy but, one day, I'll get round to publishing it. I trust that thereafter, via bookshops and libraries, it'll terrify a generous proportion of the children of the English-speaking world. Meanwhile, I hope it gives you the creeps.*

HOTEL MUSIC

(words: Nick Toczek / music: Matt Webster)

By
night,
air-con
has its fans.
They whistle.
Ventilators sigh.
A balcony launches
brief bursts of language.
Out back, trash avalanches.
Then the bin lid loudly slams.
Hot kitchens exhale an oily steam.
TVs dream or ooze ill news from wars.
Cars purr, rub up, draw their claws, pause.
Loud people pour through doors, are absorbed.
Rooms murmur. Passing planes scrape at the sky.
Out here, asthmatic, I cough, silencing the single cicada
and causing roosting birds in the planted palms to complain.
They pick up phones, call reception, are told that someone will
                                                        deal with me.

NICK: *I wrote this late one night in Qatar. I'd been for a walk, taking a notebook and pen with me. Pausing in a street next to a thick hedge which screened off one side of a busy hotel, I simply made notes about everything I could hear. Back in my hotel room, that list became this poem.*

CLOSE UP

(words: Nick Toczek / music: Matt Webster & Mark Cranmer)

Inhale, exhale; inhale, exhale.
Listen to lungs. Don't let them fail.
Weak where once they blew a gale.
Hear them whistle. How they wail.

Inhale, exhale; inhale, exhale.
These ribs are bars which built this jail.
Each breath an inmate begging bail.
There's no reprieve. No call. No mail.

Inhale, exhale; inhale, exhale.
Never known struggling on this scale.
Failure at the speed of a snail.
And, oh, it leaves a dreadful trail.

Inhale, exhale; inhale, exhale.
It's crucifixion, nail by nail.
A sacrifice beyond the pale.
A landed fish to flap, to flail.

Inhale, exhale; inhale, exhale.
One day this wind will fill our sail.
One day we'll live to tell this tale.
One day our souls won't be for sale.

NICK: *During the first year of the Covid-19 pandemic (specifically from 15 March 2020 to 15 March 2021) I wrote daily poems about what I and we were going through, publishing each on my own Facebook page and on Janine Booth's excellent CoronaVerses Facebook page. I've divided the 366 into three roughly equal collections. The first, 'Corona Diary' was published in 2020. The second, 'The Year The World Stood Still' will make its delayed appearance in the spring of 2022. A third collection, as yet untitled, will follow later in the year. This lyric was one of those poems. It was written for all those, in Britain and around the world, whose lungs were slowly failing as the virus took their lives.*

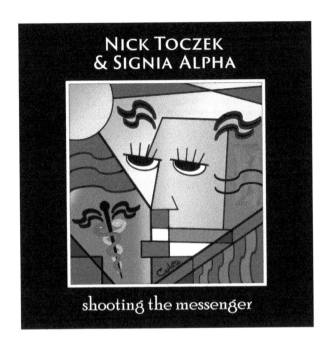

SHOOTING THE MESSENGER

SIDE 1

1. THE VOICES IN HIS HEAD (4.36) (Toczek/Webster/Cranmer)
2. NO MESSAGES (4.24) (Toczek/Webster/Atkinson)
3. WATCHING THIS CITY BY NIGHT (2.04) (Toczek/Webster)
4. WHEN WE MEN TALK (4.32) (Toczek/Webster/Cranmer)
5. THE PAINTING (4.14) (Toczek/Webster)
6. RESPONSIBILITIES (0.56) (Toczek/Webster)

SIDE 2

1. THE LIGHTER (4.55) (Toczek/Webster/Cranmer)
2. GOD HELP US (3.40) (Toczek/Webster/Atkinson)
3. THIS CITY EATS (3.44) (Toczek/Webster/Andrews/Botterell)
4. THE MAN WHO BUILT THE TITANIC (3.26) (Toczek/Webster)
5. AND A THEFT (3.19) (Toczek/Webster)
6. APPLEDORE (2.17) (Toczek/Webster)

THE VOICES IN HIS HEAD

(Nick Toczek)

My friend who trod where angels tread
Spoke of the voices in his head.
Inventions, fictions and the dead
All talked to him at night in bed.

The voices, oh, the voices, oh,
The voices in his head.

When logic, sense and reason fled,
He clung like spiders do to thread,
A person guided, driven, led
By voices anchored in his head.

The voices, oh, the voices, oh,
The voices in his head
The voices, oh, the voices, oh,
The voices in his... head.

Stampeding through his brain, there sped
A bestiary that brewed and bred
With bits from books he claimed he'd read
And these became what filled his head.

He listened, eaten up with dread,
To what this spider-web had spread:
A litany spat, shat and bled,
A blood-red nightmare in his head.

And though he heard the words we said
They came to him with meaning shed
And so he chose to heed instead
The words he heard inside his head.

This weird world to which he's wed
Becomes his butter, beef and bread,
Till all around, behind, ahead,
The undead tread within his head.

They talk and he gives them full cred.
No proof. In truth, there's none, no shred,
Yet they're his all, his a-to-zed,
The universe inside his head.

The voices, oh, the voices, oh,
The voices in his head
The voices, oh, the voices, oh,
The voices in his... head.

NICK: *A few years apart, two close friends of mine were sectioned in the same mental health facility. I visited both of them while they were there. These experiences left a deep impression on me. Though I could offer little concrete help to either of them, I strove to understand the deeply disturbing worlds which they each occupied. This lyric stems entirely from long conversations with one of the two.*

NICK TOCZEK
& SIGNIA ALPHA

the voices in his head

NO MESSAGES

(words: Nick Toczek / music: Matt Webster & Jack Atkinson)

We linger at the rendezvous.
Arrival now long overdue.
No passengers and where's the crew?
And where's the plane on which they flew?
There is no hint. We have no clue.
No messages are coming through.

        The obvious becomes taboo.
        The falsehoods form. The rumours brew.
        With hearsay, which may not be true,
        The situation's nothing new
        Yet no one knows quite what to do.
        No messages are coming through.

They've disappeared into the blue.
The evidence we misconstrue.
Conspiracies: the theories grew
Contagiously, like AIDS, like flu.
The reason is the facts are few.
No messages are coming through.

        And so it is with me and you.
        And so it is now we are through
        With what we had and what we blew.
        We're wading through the residue.
        We don't discuss. We just argue.
        No messages are coming through.

When truth tells lies and lies are true
Our wreckage lies beyond rescue.
We have no verbal avenue.
Our silences line up. Their queue
Just tells us what we always knew
No messages, no messages,
No messages are coming through.

NICK: *The broad theme of 'Shooting The Messenger' is how we receive or transmit information. While all the other lyrics were drawn from my pre-existing work, 'No Messages' was specifically written on that theme for this album. The lyric begins with people waiting, uninformed, at an airport for news of the fate of passengers on a plane that's failed to arrive on time. It ends with a dysfunctional and deteriorating personal relationship in which communication has broken down.*

Coincidentally, while we were working on this project, my mother died and left me one of her favourite possessions, knowing that I also liked it. This is a bronze statue of Mercury, fabled messenger of the Gods. Made in 1910 by the famed French sculptor, Raymond Sudre, it's well over two feet tall. Photos of it feature in the artwork of both the CD and the vinyl editions of 'Shooting The Messenger', in memory of my mum.

WATCHING THIS CITY BY NIGHT

(words: Nick Toczek / music: Matt Webster)

The thin skins ripple on puddles
As if disturbed by ghosts of this.

We're lamp-watched under winter gusts
Which fuss about like hosts of this.

See silhouettes on bicycles
Slide past the signs and posts of this.

With oceanic skies above,
Those roof-tops shape the coasts of this.

And every car which whispers past
Testifies and boasts of this.

NICK: *While visiting schools in Holland, I spent one night in The Hague. I was the sole guest in a city centre hotel. Arriving around 8 p.m. I checked in, unpacked, showered and then went down to the bar for food and a drink.*

The one member of staff still on duty served me and then said that he was going home. As the only person in the whole building, I ate in silence sitting at a table next to a soundproof glass wall below which was a main road. Beyond that was a view of the city. As I ate, I wrote this piece. Everything I saw was part of a panoramic mime. This is a poem devoid of all sound. It was as if I'd suddenly become deaf.

WHEN WE MEN TALK

(words: Nick Toczek / music: Matt Webster & Mark Cranmer)

When we men talk...

We talk because we want to, we talk because we can.
We talk about the ways to make an omelette or a flan.
We talk about the Buddhist riddle known as a koan.
We talk about all sorts of sports of which we're each a fan.
We talk about the way to be when talking man to man.
We talk about mortality, our blood-test and our scan.
We talk the kind of language which governments might ban.

When we men talk...

We talk about our family, of mum and dad and gran.
We talk as if we hardly care. We try to stay deadpan.
We talk about the job we do, our customers, our van.
We talk about our Christmases, Yom Kippur, Ramadan.
We talk about the years we spent in Russia or Japan.
We talk about our film careers in Hollywood and Cannes.
We talk about our situations, how it all began.

When we men talk...

We talk about the future and envisage some grand plan.
We talk about the wealthy, unemployed and artisan.
We talk of Myra, Mary, Mona, Meg and Marianne.
We talk about our holiday, our hotel and our tan.
We talk about the stuff we add, from salt to parmesan.
We talk about the life we've lived, the businesses we ran.
We talk to change the subject to anything other than…

WHEN WE MEN TALK RAP

(Nick Toczek)

Pens we push. Price we pay.
Pints in pubs. Swagger'n'sway.
Plain as porridge. Dense as clay.
This the stuff that we men say.

Razor blade. Rub'n'spray.
Black'n'white. Shades of grey.
Stains which we won't wash away.
This the stuff that we men say.

Grass we mow. Fields we play.
Oats we sow while making hay.
Climate change when tempers fray.
This the stuff that we men say.

Maybe versus yeah or nay.
Could be straight or could be gay.
Pagger, batter, belt or bray.
This the stuff that we men say.

Lay'n'leave or love'n'stay.
Pray for bird, get bird of prey.
Burden till our dying day.
This the stuff that we men say.

Kingdom come or come what may.
Somewhere something goes astray.
Okay, hey'n'anyway.
This the stuff that we men say.

NICK: *When men gather in a bar, their conversation often grows louder and louder. Soon everyone else in the place is subjected to their stories, opinions, arguments, jokes and all else that they're sharing. However wide-ranging their conversations become, they're seldom personal and almost never confessional, which is what I mean by the last line of this poem.*

THE PAINTING

(words: Nick Toczek / music: Matt Webster)

We painted a picture to show to our friends… the sort of picture that people can enjoy, but we left it somewhere by mistake. What happened was that we put it down for a moment. Then half-way through that moment, someone said something important and we left without it. When we went back, it had gone.

No one knew where it went. We asked everybody, described it to them in detail, let it be known that we'd give a modest reward for its return, made threats, cursed, got drunk, and shouted about its beauty, the tragedy of its loss. All this, but to no avail.

Years later, we were all dead. Still no-one let on about its whereabouts. It took centuries, whole centuries. Now, of course, anyone can see it. It's on exhibition in the main gallery of the capital city. The man who found it paid 250 for it and sold it to a dealer for 500. He was pleased to have made such a profit.

The dealer sold it to the gallery for 5,000, and now the gallery say that it's priceless. 'What a painting!' say the critics, 'What a painting!'

Long dead, our friends haunt the gallery. They listen to the hushed echoes of admiration from critics and patrons and tourists. We tell our friends that it's the painting we did for them.

They're happy that so many people appreciate it, and they wish they could see it for themselves. But the dead are blind to such inanimates. They see only each other and the living. They can do no more than watch people staring at an empty space and wish that they could see where the painting was and what it looked like.

We can't even remember ourselves what it was that we painted. But its beauty, oh, we remember that well. It was a beautiful painting.

> **NICK:** *I'd visited an art gallery not long before writing this short ghost story. While there, I'd sensed that some of the artists - all long dead - seemed almost to be there with us as we viewed their work and read the accompanying outlines of their lives.*

RESPONSIBILITIES

(words: Nick Toczek / music: Matt Webster)

Our kids who've grown and flown the nest
Now only phone us to request
More cash on loan, their tone depressed.

We're shown their debts. We've known. We've guessed.
They own mere pence. They've blown the rest.
"We're stony-broke!" they drone, distressed.

They moan. We groan, but re-invest
In those who've grown and flown the nest:
Our blood-and-bone, our own, our best.

NICK: *This tightly-composed little poem repeats the same three (-own, -own, -est) rhymes per line. I was commissioned to write it by an advertising agency. It was used in a much-broadcast TV and radio advert for The Prudential Insurance Company. We had young children at the time, and the payment (several thousand pounds) came as a financial lifeline.*

Despite selling out, I really like this poem and am particularly proud of the TV advert (which won a major advertising industry production award, and can be found on my website - www.nicktoczek.com). In that short film, the promotional text was voiced by the poet Roger McGough and my poem was read, very much as I read it, by the actor Bernard Hill.

THE LIGHTER

(words: Nick Toczek / music: Matt Webster & Mark Cranmer)

Sap rises to the leaf on which an insect settles. The wings seize the sunlight and split its spectrum of colours. The two front legs work furiously at the head and antennae for several minutes. This could be compulsive cleaning or it might be scratching.

The sun slants its heat over the late tropical afternoon, and this forest is awash with the buzz and hum of predatory animal traffic. A bird catches and snatches the insect forever from leaf and from life itself.

Leaf and tree, insect and bird fall below the earth. Time turns them all into coal – a black and tangibly total obliteration of their being. Others turn to oil.

I flick a flame from my lighter, burn the gas refined from natural fuel, light a cigarette that could contain my own death.

For a second, in the neat yellow flash of fire, I almost see the bird rise like a phoenix, a rainbow of insect wings in its beak; or it's as if I'm witnessing the foliage of a long-lost forest burning in the sunlight centuries and centuries away.

But it's gone before I draw the first lungful of smoke. And already I feel the impatience of time, its vortex drawing my own flesh and bone beyond life and down towards earth and coal and tar. There is a sense of the self, dissolving into smoke, in the lungs of the eternal.

> **NICK:** *Though I haven't smoked since the early 1980s, I still often cast myself as a heavy smoker in vivid recurring dreams. In one of these, I'm standing in a windy winter street, coat collar turned up, trying unsuccessfully to light a cigarette. Transferring that moment to a tropical forest, I wrote this short story about mortality.*

GOD HELP US

(words: Nick Toczek / music: Matt Webster & Jack Atkinson)

And God gets impatient. "We done yet?" he asks
Grown pig-sick of listening, exhausted by tasks.
His damned omnipresence gives no getaway.
No lunch-break. No weekend. No brief holiday.
Eternity tells him that he's here to stay.

Thrown praise, prayers and sung to, with zero relief,
He's held like a hostage, bound by blind belief,
Implored without end to arrange the unplanned
And change the unchanging with his mighty hand.
He simply can't do that. They don't understand.

All-seeing, all-knowing… okay, he's all that
But he doesn't pull rabbits out of his hat.
Creation's an art, not a form of magic,
And raising the dead is no everyday trick.
It's hard enough healing a human who's sick.

While his still small voice seems like it goes unheard
Their clamour – like tinnitus – rings loud and blurred.
That wailing and moaning worm under his skin.
There's no insulating himself from their din.
He curses their suffering and curses their sin.

There's no job as tough as this deity bizz.
The grinding and gnashing of teeth are all his.
In retrospect he finds it hard to believe
That there was a time when he'd goals to achieve
Till he went and blew it with Adam and Eve.

NICK: *I'd hate to be God. The job's unrewarding and the hours are lousy. I bet he wishes he was a poet.*

THIS CITY EATS

(words: Nick Toczek / music: Webster, Andrews, Botterell)

This city eats, this city eats, this city eats itself

Shovels down its ancient stone,
Dines on human flesh and bone,
Steals from mates it's always known:
Laptop, TV, mobile phone.
Neighbourhood's a no-go zone.
"Gotcha!" screams your sick ringtone.

This city eats, this city eats, this city eats itself

Come the king without a crown,
City crumbles, tumbles down.
One-time wonder turned to clown,
Painted grin to growing frown.
Business now begins to drown.
Cut-backs kill this crippled town.

This city eats, this city eats, this city eats itself

Swallows everything it's got,
Cash is hot, compassion's not,
Trashes every vacant lot,
Tears all down for building plot,
Stands back, lets its history rot,
Shoots up, shits up, should be shot.

This city eats, this city eats, this city eats itself

No defence, a naked goal,
Cannibal with begging bowl
Pays the price out on parole,
Digs 'n' drags through drug, debt, dole,
Turned to meat 'n' eaten whole,
Skewered through its urban soul.

This city eats, this city eats, this city eats itself

Bites its brickwork, chews concrete,
Bones of buildings stripped of meat,
Drags dead rain straight up main street.
Shops shut down, troops in retreat,
All that's new lies incomplete,
Assets gone, there's no receipt.

This city eats, this city eats, this city eats itself.

NICK: *This was written about fifteen years ago about my Yorkshire home town of Bradford. It's a city I love. I was born here in 1950 and still live here more than seventy years later.*

During the 1960s, its main industry of textiles went into catastrophic decline. Throughout the seventies and Thatcherite eighties, unemployment and poverty reduced it to a shadow of it's once-prosperous self. A partial recovery during the nineties was dramatically reversed when the despicable multinational company, Westfield, dug up the entire city centre for a planned shopping mall and then abandoned the project for the next fifteen years, leaving the heart of the city as a vast fenced-in mess of mud and part-built foundations. I wrote this in rage at what they'd done to our city, its culture and its people.

THE MAN WHO BUILT THE TITANIC

(words: Nick Toczek / music: Matt Webster)

The man who built The Titanic never talks about oceans and has a morbid fear of the cold.

His recurring dream is panoramic. Eskimo sailors steer a ship of ice through seas of scrap metal. Every sound echoes dull and heavy through fog and the captain is perpetually drunk.

The dreamer peers over the side of the ship. The seabed is a mile below, and he can make out fronds of metal weed curling up towards him.

The people who are going to jump when the panic starts will simply drop like stones. There's no water to catch them here.

As the band stops playing, he can feel the great hull of ice start to shudder, and hears the drawn out groan as it cracks apart.

Asleep, he keels over in bed, grinding his teeth hard, a sound that fills his head like ice shearing on metal. The man who built The Titanic lives near the Equator and seldom takes a bath.

 His house smells of him, except the kitchen. Here, without a fridge, food rots quickly in the heat, and the stench attracts gulls.

They wheel and screech in the air above his house and, when he throws out the garbage, they dive onto the deck, and fight like people in a panic.

NICK: *We've all experienced the gnawing persistence of guilt. Here's a short story that focuses on someone with good cause to be thus plagued.*

AND A THEFT

(words: Nick Toczek / music: Matt Webster)

And after dusk, and in the deserted library, the night is a small black book through which no one ever looks. I pocket it, leave as quickly and quietly as I came.

The pages are cold and silent against my hip, but the stars are metallic and pass for coinage. They pay for my bus ticket.

I sit upstairs, let slip an accidental handful of owls. These settle on the seat-backs and stare me out, eyes huge with accusations.

And on the walk home, and then in my dreams, and out across the surface of my wakening, and even in the daylight: moths.

They follow me everywhere because my clothes, because my body, because my thinking, because all of these and everything I touch and everywhere I go adopt the odour of moonlight. This they follow because they are moths and because the moon has never been so close.

And all my clothes are black and heavy, and I cannot undress, and I have no pockets, and my hands are full of high cloud, and I cannot touch the book, and my body is thinned by night air, and my head is a void of echoes and distances, and the carpet fills with pins of light that are cities caught up in a mesh of sleep…

… all of which pulls away, beyond the odour of moonlight, beyond the taste of planets, beyond the texture of stars, until everything has been stolen, and the theft is complete.

NICK: *Here's another short tale, this time about the enormous consequences of a minor crime. Really, it's about how an action can play back on you in unimaginably magnified form.*

APPLEDORE

(words: Nick Toczek / music: Matt Webster)

Drowned sailors lie in St. Mary's Graveyard, in the Devon
fishing village of Appledore.

Lifted from the water, lain below the ground
Long lie the many men, lured from land and drowned.
Birdsong lulls my footfall. They hear neither sound.
Flesh and cares have fled from dull bones bared and browned.
Silent strands like sea weeds wrap them round and round.
Tides of time now trap them near where waves still pound.
These the seas that left them lifeless, lost then found
Borne ashore by mourners, stored where all are bound,

The graveyard, Appledore.

NICK: *St Mary's Graveyard in the lovely Devon
fishing village of Appledore is just a couple of
hundred yards from the seafront. It contains many
graves of men who were drowned when their fishing
boats were lost at sea. I tour Devon schools every
autumn as part of the annual Appledore Children's
Book Festival, staying at The Seagate Hotel which is
just round the corner from this quiet graveyard.*

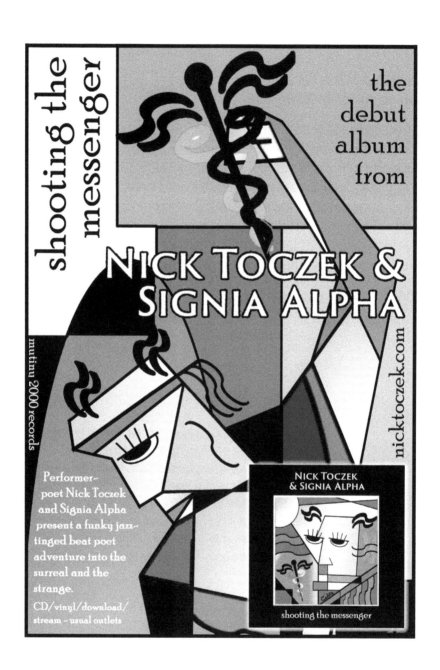

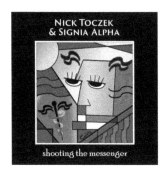

SHOOTING THE MESSENGER CD

1. THE VOICES IN HIS HEAD (5.36) (Toczek/Webster/Cranmer)

2. NO MESSAGES (4.23) (Toczek/Webster/Atkinson)

3. QUIET RIOT(4.22) (Toczek/Webster/Cranmer/Jafrate/Williams)

4. WATCHING THIS CITY BY NIGHT (2.02) (Toczek/Webster)

5. WHEN WE MEN TALK (6.00) (Toczek/Webster/Cranmer)

6. THE PAINTING (4.11) (Toczek/Webster)

7. GOD HELP US (3.40) (Toczek/Webster/Atkinson)

8. THE MAN WHO BUILT THE TITANIC (3.26) (Toczek/Webster)

9. THIS CITY EATS (3.45) (Toczek/Webster/Andrews/Botterell)

10. THE LIGHTER (5.56) (Toczek/Webster/Cranmer)

11. RESPONSIBILITIES (0.52) (Toczek/Webster)

12. MAN ON A TRAIN (3.51) (Toczek/Webster)

13. THE POEM I WROTE ABOUT YOU (2.23) (Toczek/Atkinson/Webster)

14. STIFF WITH A QUIFF (4.21) (Toczek/Webster/Jafrate)

15. AND A THEFT (3.19) (Toczek/Webster)

16. SCARS (4.12) (Toczek/Webster/Andrews)

17. APPLEDORE (2.30) (Toczek/Webster)

QUIET RIOT

(words: Nick Toczek / music: Cranmer, Jafrate, Webster)

We riot in our quiet streets
Suburban scum, we dumb elites
Lob angry emails, texts and tweets
While coppers stroll by on their beats
We riot in our quiet streets

With nobody to photo-take
And no political earthquake
No Arab Spring. No windows break
While dieting, for Heaven's sake

We riot in our quiet streets
While reading Shelley, Wordsworth, Keats
We pay for stuff and get receipts
And chewing gum and eating sweets
We riot in our quiet streets

While mums are baking birthday cake
And bread-fed ducks park on the lake
Our home-grown revolution's fake
So knowing there's no life at stake

We riot in our quiet streets
Though no one gets up from their seats
While TV stations screen repeats
But ruled by liars, thieves and cheats
We riot in our quiet streets

Then tidy up what mess we make
So all's shipshape when we next wake
And those who don't take part partake
And though the cause now seems opaque

We riot in our quiet streets
While, out at sea, we're losing fleets
And daily learn of new defeats
Though all we hang are laundered sheets
We riot in our quiet streets

And when things burn, it's by mistake
Black smoke from barbecuing steak
We mow the lawn. We hoe. We rake
The boredom makes us bellyache

We riot in our quiet streets
Where, like some shark, the darkness eats
And sinks its teeth in human meats
So peace won't come to these retreats
We riot in our quiet streets

Where Crimewatch keeps us all awake
Its nightmares stories make us shake
And rattle us just like a snake
Or vampire with a thirst to slake

We riot in our quiet streets
Then bag up shit the dog excretes
And sit and beg like him for treats
We snarling sheep, our barks are bleats
We riot in our quiet streets.

NICK: *Here's a lyric mocking middle-class and middle-aged suburban British 'revolutionaries'. When I wrote it, I was aiming it at myself as well as others like me who find it all too easy to let home comforts restrict political activism.*

MAN ON A TRAIN

(words: Nick Toczek / music: Matt Webster)

The man on the early train sees the sun rise, arthritic, and slant a few fine squints of watery light towards him along the dusty surface of an end-of-October landscape.

It conjures this picture: of an old man, crumpled fingers clutching the edge of a hospital table, puckering the cloth. His mouth hangs open and he's waiting for the nurse to bring him food. He hunches, head hung between his shoulders just above table level. And he is what he seems to be: a sun on its horizon.

There's a familiar noise in the distance. The old man tries to remember what causes it, and tries to place it. It moves slowly across the far side of the tablecloth. He stares after it through watery eyes. The cutlery, cups and pots become industrial structures under his failing gaze. The creases in the cloth form divisions: walls, roads, hedges… and now he knows that noise.

It's a train. As a child, he'd stir in bed after dawn and hear it hammer down the valley with its load of post, papers and early risers. Now, the table-top train thunders along the rim of his vision.

All those years ago, he'd have leapt out from under warm blankets onto the cold shock of polished floor, padded across bare boards to the window, and watched it go – steam then, diesel now – sailing away. He might even (leaning in blue-and-white pyjamas over the sill and into the icy air) have been seen by the man on board.

So the two of them would watch while the rising sun struggled, ancient and open-mouthed, groping forward with spidery fingers of light across a misted landscape that has become the vast spread of time between the one person who was all three… child, commuter and old man.

> **NICK:** *All three characters in this short story are me. Written back in the 1980s, this piece remembers me as a child in the fifties, and then as a man on a train some thirty years later. The third character in this piece, is my imagined decrepit self, the very person I'm now well on the way to becoming.*

THE POEM I WROTE ABOUT YOU

(words: Nick Toczek / music: Jack Atkinson & Matt Webster)

I didn't write one, I actually wrote two.
And then there were others. I wrote quite a few.
I tried to keep count but the numbers just grew.
So those were the poems I wrote about you
Because I'm a poet and that's what we do.

And, when they'd been written, I sent them to you.
The Post Office told me that they'd all got through
Which I knew and you knew and they knew was true:
Anonymous poems from someone you knew
Though you hardly cared that you didn't know who.

You asked a few friends but they hadn't a clue.
You got lots of poems. Mine just joined the queue.
Yet such stuff was something from which you withdrew
The way that some people are frightened of flu
Or spiders or clowns or what cannibals do.

You never read poems, not even haiku.
Averse to all verse, your antipathy grew.
Some people, they're like that, and you joined their crew
And anyhow you'd other things to pursue
Like Pernod and pretzels and trips to Peru.

So, off on your travels, you bid us adieu.
As they say in France, parley-voo. Entre nous
Those poems, unread and long rendered taboo
Were missed off the list of what you took with you.
You'd yesterday flushed the whole lot down the loo.

NICK: *I don't write many love poems. As a tongue-in-cheek tale of unrequited love, this is about as near as I usually get to being a romantic poet.*

STIFF WITH A QUIFF

(words: Nick Toczek / music: Matt Webster & Keith Jafrate)

Half-past-six with a belly full of grub
Stiff with a quiff quits home for the pub.
Seven to eleven in the public bar:
"We're here for the beer and a laugh – Ha-Ha!"
He's wed to a flooze but they hardly speak
So he hits the booze most nights of the week.

"And it's a lousy life," she thinks.
"It's a lousy life. It stinks."

Flatulent, fat and forty, fortified,
He's put fourteen pints of bitter inside.
Nowt in his pockets as he staggers home
But a packet of fags and a greasy comb.
He slams the door, kicks off his shoes
And is fast asleep before the tea brews.

"And it's a lousy life," she thinks.
"It's a lousy life. It stinks."

She looks at beery slumped in his chair.
Call it a marriage? There's bugger-all there.
An hour more telly to drunken snores.
What with him and the box and the household chores,
Home's a hopeless habit, like heroin,
The needle stuck firmly under her skin.

"And it's a lousy life," she thinks.
"It's a lousy life. It stinks."

It's a lousy life for the washed-up wife
Of a permanently plastered
permanently plastered
permanently plastered pissed up
pissed up
pissed up bastard...
bastard...
bastard.

SCARS

(words: Nick Toczek / music: Matt Webster & Stephen Andrews)

These are the regions of hatred and pain
Pieces of days that we cannot contain
This is the burning returning again
Wounds which have healed yet their shadows remain

After the cleansing there'll still be a stain
Sins are forgiven but grudges ingrain
Tattooed forever deep inside your brain
Faraway songs with a snagging refrain

Judgements delivered to drive us from sane
Atmospheres lingering long after rain
Items of evidence buried in vain
Surfacing shrapnel our bodies retain.

NICK: *Here's a dark poem about the hurt we can inflict on ourselves and our partners within an otherwise loving relationship. It's probably the most honest poem I've ever written.*

STIFF WITH A QUIFF: *This poem / lyric about a woman with a drunken husband has served me well, not least when, without my permission, Pete Doherty, singer-songwriter of the band Babyshambles, used the last few lines as the chorus of 'Baddies Boogie', one of the band's most popular songs. After five years of legal wrangling, I got half-ownership of the song, was paid several thousand pounds and still receive quarterly royalty payments. You can find the full story on my website.*

COMING TO GET YOU NEXT

(words: Nick Toczek / music: Matt Webster)

We warned you all. We sent a text
That you'd be cursed, that you'd be hexed.
They're coming to getcha, coming to getcha,
Coming to getcha next.

They got your vote. You look perplexed.
You put them there, so don't be vexed.
They're coming to getcha, coming to getcha,
Coming to getcha next.

They're overpaid and undersexed.
With muscle now which must be flexed.
They're coming to getcha, coming to getcha,
Coming to getcha next.

With weasel words, their diplomat
'll worm across your welcome mat
And right inside your habitat –

Your heart, your home, your house, your flat.
They're coming to getcha, coming to getcha,
Coming to getcha next.
I said they're coming to getcha,
Coming to getcha, coming to getcha next.

They'll tell you this. They'll yell you that.
They'll sell you loads of lies and tat
And play the verbal acrobat
And shower you in golden chat.
They're coming to getcha, coming to getcha,
Coming to getcha next.

I said they're coming to getcha, coming to getcha,
Coming to getcha next.

They'll wash your brain. Their Laundromat
'll saturate those cells in fat
And fill you full of shit they shat
And sit you back where you were sat.
They're coming to getcha, coming to getcha,
Coming to getcha next.
I said they're coming to getcha, coming to getcha,
Coming to getcha next.

You can't combat a bureaucrat
Who'll have you choke on your own hat
And make you pay and charge you VAT
And, treat you like a total twat.

They're coming to getcha, coming to getcha,
Coming to getcha next.
I said they're coming to getcha, coming to getcha,
Coming to getcha next.
Yeah, they're coming to getcha, coming to getcha,
Coming to getcha next.
They're… coming to getcha, coming to getcha,
Coming to getcha next.

NON-ALBUM SINGLE

NICK: *Inspired by Pastor Martin Niemoller's poem 'First They Came', I wrote this poem / lyric about manipulative governments back in the early 1990s. It's even more pertinent now.*

PART 2: THE MUSIC

A FEW SANDS FROM THE HOUR GLASS

By Matt Webster

Since Nick and I started working on these albums, I have often been asked how we match the lyrics to the music, as we unconventionally set spoken word to rock or jazz or funk.

We aren't the first to do this, of course. My inspiration stems from some of my biggest musical influences who've occasionally dabbled in the form. These include The Clash (*Magnificent Seven*), The Stranglers (*Peaches*), The Jam (*Pop Art Poem*), Ian Dury, Blondie (*Rapture*), David Bowie (*Future Legend*), as well as Gill Scott Heron's *The Revolution Will Not Be Televised*.

Another big inspiration was the collaboration between San Franciscan hip hop duo The Disposable Heroes of Hiphoprisy and beat poet William S. Burroughs on the album *Spare Ass Annie and Other Tales*, where surreal stories are read over a hip hop backing.

Before we go any further, it might be best to press rewind and explain what led up to the making of these albums.

I met Nick in 1983 when he was promoting punk gigs at venues in Bradford, Leeds and Keighley. At that time I was in a fledgling hardcore punk band called The Convulsions. Bass player Kenny Armitage and I used to regularly accost Nick at these gigs in an attempt to get him to give our fabulous band a support slot. Eventually, he gave in and offered us two gigs, the first supporting The Subhumans and The Instigators on a notorious night at The Vaults Bar in Bradford, and later in a multi-band New Year's gig at The Bier Keller in Leeds.

Winding forward to 1997, I was in the final line-up of a band called Zed. We rented a rehearsal space on the top floor of a mill on Thornton Road in Bradford which later became a nightclub (The Mill). At that time, the top floor was an open space apart from an already built unit occupied by the legendary Bradford psychedelic DJ and light show that was, and still is, Griff's Magic Theatre.

The mill was owned by Ally Briggs who had a print workshop on the first floor. Next to this, he had built a small eight-track recording studio which Zed used to record an album that summer. We called the album *Mutiny 2000*. The name came about after Zed had played a 'Unity 1997' event at Sussex Arts Centre in Brighton. A friend of ours referred to this as 'Mutiny 1997' which became 'Mutiny 2000'.

Although happy with our performances on the album, we were disappointed with the sound of what had been put down on tape. I was certain that I could do a better job of capturing the initial sound of the instruments, particularly the drums, so we built walls around our rehearsal space to create a place in which we could also record.

In 1996, I had a stupid, drunken accident with a very sharp knife which severed the nerves and tendon in my left index finger. After an operation to re-attach my tendon, I was forced to wear a metal brace on my hand. Designed to prevent my left hand from moving, it felt like someone was continually trying to break my wrist for the next three months. This was followed by another few months where I could hardly use my hand. My index finger has never fully recovered.

I had always taken a keen interest in the recording and mixing process when I'd recorded with my bands, so I took this time to learn more about recording and mixing. I took a course in studio recording at the Engine Rooms studio in Bradford before starting a two-year Music Technology course at Bradford College. In 1998, Zed guitarist Crispian Baker developed cluster headaches, a debilitating neurological condition that sadly led to his death in 2015. This was another reason Jont (Zed frontman and bassist) and I shifted focus from the band to create a studio and label.

Aided and abetted by like-minded musician friends (notably Mark 'Moota' Appleyard, Harris, Chad Meade, Robert Heaton and, later, Simon Mawson and James Atkinson), we pooled gear and skills to build and equip a pretty decent studio. It had a 32-channel mixing desk and a 16-track analogue tape machine. It seemed appropriate to name our studio and label after the album that had led to its creation; Mutiny 2000.

By the year 2000, the top floor of The Mill had become a hive of activity, housing other units used by Bradford's New Model Army and Leeds tubthumpers Chumbawamba. It was also the year our studio was fully up and running.

Over the next few years, we recorded and released a series of CD albums on Mutiny 2000 Records. There were two compilations of new music by bands using the studio. These albums were mainly recorded by Rob Heaton and me and compiled by the two of us and Jont. The first, *White Abbey Road*, was promoted by a gig in the cellar nightclub at The Mill where every band on the album played. We also compiled and released albums by bands we'd previously been involved in, among them Zed, Psycho Surgeons, Requiem, The Horton Carpets, Western Dance and Primate. Rob and I also edited and repaired old recordings for New Model Arny's *Lost Songs* double CD compilation. There were also new albums by Moota, Jazz Mutiny, Angelo Palladino and Kwai Chang Caine.

Several grains of sand later, in 2007, Nick approached me to remaster and re-release his 11-track 1987 vinyl album *InTOCZEKated* as a CD which included a further 14 tracks drawn from his recorded history of working with a wide variety of bands and musicians. This CD was released that year on Mutiny 2000 Records as *Totally InTOCZEKated*.

Shortly after, my life took a devastating turn. In 1997, a long-term problem with back pain turned out to be the debilitating arthritic spinal disease, Ankylosing Spondylitis, which steadily worsened over the next decade. In December 2007, I experienced a massive flare-up which hit me with a wave of unimaginable agony, causing me to be hospitalised. An initial misdiagnosis led to me being housed in an infectious disease ward which seemingly gathered together all the worst diseases known to man in one convenient place. It was during that nightmare stay I discovered that a spinal tap is not just the name of a fictitious band. Through a haze of morphine, I remember finding that point very amusing, just before they stuck a very large needle into my spine.

After being released from hospital, I was bedridden for months, surviving on a diet of morphine and sleeping pills. The late diagnosis meant that the treatment I should have had was delayed by months and this has left me with a permanently fused spine. Since then, every eight weeks, I need to have an IV drip infusion which knocks out my immune system to keep me at least partially mobile.

For almost a decade after that, I gave up any hopes of ever playing music again. For the next nine years, my only music-related endeavour was the co-writing of a series of books about local music history called *Bradford's Noise Of The Valleys*, the concept of my co-writer and friend, Gary Cavanagh, who was a founder of Bradford's 1 In 12 Club. For this project, we have, to date, compiled and released sixteen CDs of Bradford-related bands and acts from the sixties, seventies and eighties, as companion collections to the books.

2016 saw the thirtieth anniversary of the formation of my old band, Western Dance, and a reunion gig was proposed. To my great joy and surprise, I found I could still sit at and play a drum kit. It was, in fact, much easier for me than standing or walking. The anniversary gig went well and left me keen to carry on playing.

Around this time, my old friend (and cousin by marriage), Mark Cranmer, had joined a blues-rock covers combo called The Johnny Gray Band. They were rehearsing in an old mill which happened to be just opposite the original Mutiny 2000 studio. Mark had set up a mixing desk and recording facilities where they rehearsed. When their drummer left, in November, I was invited to join.

Along with rediscovering my passion for playing the drums, my interest in recording was also rekindled. I invested in some Shure drum mics and bought a Soundcraft mixing desk. The addition of some recording software and too many audio plug-ins to mention resulted in a well-equipped home mixing and recording studio. This set-up, vastly superior to the original Mutiny 2000 mixing room, is the one used for all the Nick Toczek & Signia Alpha recordings.

Back in 2017, I began recording our covers bands for promo purposes and doing some recording tests at home. Under the name Signia Alpha, I did fairly decent solo cover versions of The Stranglers' *Nice 'n' Sleazy* and *The Call Up* and *The Guns Of Brixton* by The Clash plus a couple of my own tunes.

Why that name? I'd loved Premier drums ever since seeing them played by The Jam's Rick Butler, Blondie's Clem Burke and, of course, Keith Moon. Back in the eighties, Rat Scabies of The Damned had played a Premier Black Shadow Resonator drum kit. I'd thought that was the coolest looking kit ever. Then, in the mid-nineties, came the even more desirable Premier Signia. Having since got good deals on both kits, I still slightly prefer the sound of the Signia. Hence, Signia Alpha. And, in a world where there are few unused band names, I thought that one wasn't too bad.

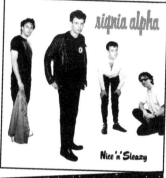

In 2018, Nick asked me to build a website through which he could promote himself and his performances, his work in schools, and his many books and recordings. I suggested that he should also use it as a platform for his past work and, in particular, an account of the punk and other rock gigs he ran during the eighties and the many alternative cabaret gigs he ran in the late eighties and early nineties.

So it came about that I was recording my music in a studio setting at home while working with Nick on his website. I thought it would be fun to get him to record some of his more surreal poems and stories over the music that I was starting to create. He agreed. Thus we began the project which became Nick Toczek & Signia Alpha.

So, how do we match the words to the music? Sometimes it's an easy task, although sometimes we go through a few possibilities first. When I was working with Rob Heaton years before, he used to describe music in colours, as in, 'that's a red song' or 'this one is purple'. I never quite saw music in that way but now I kind of know what he meant. To me, music has an atmosphere, a hue that is suggestive of a theme or mood. The words, therefore, have to suit the mood of the music or visa versa.

As most of our recordings begin with the music, I usually try to put the mood into words for Nick, i.e., 'this is a nighttime one', 'this one is industrial', 'this is about time', etc. I like to think that we get the right match between the words and the music, at least most of the time.

SHOOTING THE MESSENGER

Produced by Matt Webster and Nick Toczek.

Mixed and recorded by Matt Webster.

Recorded 2018, 2019 at Signia Alpha Studios.

Released January 1 2020 on CD and download.

Released July 4 2020 on purple vinyl.

Mutiny 2000 Records M2KSA01

THE VOICES IN HIS HEAD

(words: Nick Toczek / music: Matt Webster & Mark Cranmer)

Nick Toczek - vocals
Matt Webster - guitars, drums, keyboards, bongos
Mark Cranmer - bass
Keith Jafrate - saxophone
Emmanuel Williams - lead guitar

The backing for this song came from a session in the summer of 2019. I was on the drums and Mark Cranmer was playing bass. From this session, we got the rhythm tracks for three of the songs on the album. Mark and I had just been in a rock and blues covers band (Lenin Black) in which we did a great version of Stevie Wonder's *Superstition*. In our version, Mark played a funky slap bassline that I locked in with on the drums. I was keen to capture something in that vein for a couple of tracks on our album. I played various steady funk grooves that Mark jammed along to on bass.

Using my home studio set-up, I added bongos and a wah-wah guitar. Nick had a great lyric that fitted well which we recorded next. I edited the track into a tighter arrangement with a repeating chorus before Keith's sax was put down in the main studio. The lead guitar runs were played and recorded by Emmanuel Williams.

We chose this as our debut single, released in November 2019.

NO MESSAGES

(words: Nick Toczek / music: Matt Webster & Jack Atkinson)

Nick Toczek - vocals
Matt Webster - drums, bass
Jack Atkinson - guitar
Chris Walsh - flute

This is one of three tracks that sprang out of a session with guitarist Jack Atkinson. Jack had asked me to record and play the drums on a song he had written. While working on his track, I was sure the two of us could come up with a couple of interesting bits and pieces that could be used for the *Shooting The Messenger* album. I played a drum pattern I was keen to use while Jack improvised a riff over the top. I added a bass guitar before Nick recorded his vocals. I went to town a bit on the editing and delays to give it a kind of dub feel. Chris's flute part was the finishing touch.

WATCHING THIS CITY BY NIGHT

(words: Nick Toczek / music: Matt Webster)

Nick Toczek - vocals
Matt Webster - drums, percussion, bass, mandolin
Keith Jafrate - saxophone
Chris Walsh - flute

This song was originally just a drumbeat with some added percussion that I did as a recording test to which Nick added his vocal. It almost stayed as just drums and vocal but I later decided it would work better if I added a bassline and some mandolins. This is the first track that both Keith Jafrate and Chris Walsh play on, recorded at different times.

WHEN WE MEN TALK

(words: Nick Toczek / music: Matt Webster & Mark Cranmer)

Nick Toczek - vocals
Matt Webster - drums, percussion, guitars
Mark Cranmer - bass

Keith Jafrate - saxophone
Dee Bo General - vocals

This second track from the drum and bass session with Mark has a similar feel to *Voices*. I added bongos and guitar before Keith played his sax part. After we had recorded the main vocal, Nick wrote a rap for Dee Bo to perform.

THE PAINTING
(words: Nick Toczek / music: Matt Webster)

Nick Toczek - vocals
Matt Webster - guitars, bass, keyboards, cymbal
Chris Walsh - flute

A well-known internet shopping outlet had just delivered a Jim Dunlop Cry Baby wah-wah pedal to me and I wanted to try it out. I plugged in my Gordon Smith G2 guitar and recorded the chord sequence pretty much straight off as a test. Listening back, I thought it was the basis for a decent track and laid down a bassline and some keyboards. I loved Nick's ancient ghost story and felt it fitted the mood of the music perfectly. Chris's flute added to the ghostly atmosphere.

RESPONSIBILITIES
(words: Nick Toczek / music: Matt Webster)

Nick Toczek - vocals
Matt Webster - mandolin
Chris Walsh - flute

There was a TV advert in the 1990s with a pretty cool poem read over film of kids dropping money in the street. I remember being surprised to see the name 'Nick Toczek' pop up at the end. It turned out that the poem was read by eighties icon Yosser Hughes from *Boys From The Blackstuff* or, if you prefer, the noble King Theoden from *The Lord Of The Rings* films, otherwise known as actor Bernard Hill. I suggested we do a 'cover version' in an attempt to trigger some publicity or recognition in album reviews. My simple mandolin tune, complemented by Chris's flute, could, perhaps, have once rung out in the hall of Edoras, in Rohan or, less likely, on a boombox in the back of a transit van on the way to tarmac a road outside 1980s Liverpool.

THE LIGHTER

(words: Nick Toczek / music: Matt Webster & Mark Cranmer)

Nick Toczek - vocals
Matt Webster - drums, percussion, guitars
Mark Cranmer - bass
Keith Jafrate - saxophone
Chris Walsh - flute

This is the third song on the album that began with me on drums and Mark on bass. I also used my new wah wah pedal on this one. This is the second track with both sax and flute playing incidental parts and some solo improvisation at the end. Another surreal story from Nick and the track was complete. This track is a minute longer on the original CD version.

GOD HELP US

(words: Nick Toczek / music: Matt Webster & Jack Atkinson)

Nick Toczek - vocals
Matt Webster - drums, bass
Jack Atkinson - guitar
Chris Walsh - flute

Another track from the first session with Jack Atkinson. On this one, I set off with a kind of groove I thought The Band might have jammed while he played an appropriate spaced-out bluesy guitar. I added bass and edited it into some structure. Nick's religious text and another lovely bit of flute by Chris finished it off. Are we the pioneers of 21st Century dub-blues? Only time will tell...

THIS CITY EATS

(words: Nick Toczek / music: Matt Webster, Stephen Andrews & Jonny Botterell)

Nick Toczek - vocals
Matt Webster - drums, keyboards
Stephen Andrews - guitar
Jonny Botterell - bass

Guitarist Stephen Andrews and I have played together for many years, on rather than off, since December 1985, in bands Western Dance, Primate, Kwai Chang Caine and in a line-up of Zed. More recently, in 2018, I joined a reformed version of his punk/new wave covers band Plastic Letters, where we revel in the music of Adam & The Ants, The Clash, The Stranglers, The Specials, The Ruts, Buzzcocks, The Damned, Blondie, The Jam etc. (strictly 1976-1981 period, mind!).

This track came at the end of a session where we recorded a couple of Steve's songs for another project we were developing. With the tape still rolling, we jammed a couple of things hoping to capture something usable for the album. This one, driven by Jonny Botterell's bassline, seemed to work. After Nick recorded his vocals, I added some keyboards to finish it off.

THE MAN WHO BUILT THE TITANIC

(words: Nick Toczek / music: Matt Webster)

Nick Toczek - vocals
Matt Webster - keyboards, programming, acoustic guitar, drums

This is the oldest piece of music on the album, written and recorded in 1998. It was my attempt at a Beatles-style score, done on a midi keyboard. My original acoustic guitar demo, recorded on a four-track cassette recorder in my flat in Great Horton, Bradford, can be heard in the middle section. I had recently rediscovered this recording on an old DAT tape and thought it would be a good backing for one of Nick's surreal stories. I added a live military-style snare and bass drum after Nick recorded his vocals.

AND A THEFT

(words: Nick Toczek / music: Matt Webster)

Nick Toczek - vocals
Matt Webster - drums, bass, acoustic guitar, mandolin
Keith Jafrate - saxophone

This one grew from a front room recording test of my recently acquired 1960s Premier Royal Ace COB snare drum, played with brushes, over which I had added some heavily reverbed acoustic guitar. After recording Nick's surreal story, I came up with a bassline to give some structure to the track. The last thing to go on before the version on the CD release was Keith's sax. When I was remixing songs for the vinyl LP, I thought this one needed something else and played some mandolin parts.

APPLEDORE

(words: Nick Toczek / music: Matt Webster)

Nick Toczek - vocals
Matt Webster - bass

While messing about on my Epiphone EB3 bass one Sunday morning, I came up with a simple hymn-like sequence. I quickly recorded a couple of takes of my bassline. One of these I bathed in reverb and pushed into the background to make it sound like it was played in a vast hall or cathedral. I played my new tune to Nick over the phone and he liked it. He told me he had the perfect poem for it and came around the next day to record it.

EXTRA TRACKS ON THE CD AND DOWNLOAD CARD

QUIET RIOT
(words: Nick Toczek / music: Mark Cranmer, Keith Jafrate, Emmanuel Williams & Matt Webster)

Nick Toczek - vocals
Matt Webster - drums
Mark Cranmer - bass
Keith Jafrate - saxophone
Emmanuel Williams - guitar

This track was one of several jam pieces recorded at a reunion of jazz band The Moon, recorded by Mark, the story of which is told elsewhere in this book. I selected a suitable section of the original ten-minute live performance to work with. I experimented with the arrangement at the editing stage after Nick had recorded his vocals.

MAN ON A TRAIN
(words: Nick Toczek / music: Matt Webster)

Nick Toczek - vocals
Matt Webster - drums, acoustic guitars, bass

This one began as an experiment of mine that I felt was something to do with transport and Nick had a story that fitted with the theme. The snare drum is intended to suggest travelling over rail tracks; the bass drum, at parts and near the end, might be a heartbeat.

THE POEM I WROTE ABOUT YOU
(words: Nick Toczek / music: Matt Webster & Jack Atkinson)

Nick Toczek - vocals
Matt Webster - drums, voices
Jack Atkinson - guitar

This is the intro section to Jack Atkinson's song. The whole piece is something of a six-minute epic which we finished in another session. I thought our first attempts at the intro would make a strong backing in itself and compiled three takes before recording Nick's vocal.

STIFF WITH A QUIFF
(words: Nick Toczek / music: Matt Webster & Keith Jafrate)

Nick Toczek - vocals
Matt Webster - drums, guitar, bass, mandolin
Keith Jafrate - saxophone

After a session in the studio when we recorded all Keith's sax for the album, there was still some time left. We had a jam with the unusual line-up of sax, drums and vocals and came up with three or four half-decent recordings. I particularly wanted to use this one because of the history of the lyric (told elsewhere by Nick). Over the live drums, sax and vocals, I came up with a guitar pattern that I played in a loose and slightly drunken style, which I felt was in keeping with the lyrics (well, that's my excuse...).

SCARS
(words: Nick Toczek / music: Matt Webster & Stephen Andrews)

Nick Toczek - vocals
Matt Webster - drums, bass
Stephen Andrews - guitar

This one began with my circular tom tom-driven beat over which Steve improvised guitar.

COMING TO GET YOU NEXT
(words: Nick Toczek / music: Matt Webster)

Nick Toczek - vocals
Matt Webster - keyboards, guitar, bass, drums
Keith Jafrate - saxophone

A dance type thing that didn't seem to fit on the album, so we left it as a stand-alone single.

WALKING THE TIGHTROPE

Produced by Matt Webster and Nick Toczek.

Mixed and recorded by Matt Webster.

Recorded in January, February (before lockdown), August & September (during Bradford's brief respite from lockdown) 2020, at Signia Alpha Studio B, (late of) Try Mills, Thornton Road, Bradford.

Wulf's guitar parts recorded by himself in far off Bootle.
Mark's bass on Moon Above The Mövenpick and Hotel Music recorded by himself in far off Cornwall.
Paul Gray's bass on Best Wishes recorded by himself in far off Wales.
Nogsy's guitar parts recorded by himself in far-off Sheffield.
Drums and guitars on Moon Above The Mövenpick and Hotel Music recorded in 2018.
Mixed and overdubs recorded at Signia Alpha Studio A, Bradford, 2020.

Released March 31 2021 on transparent yellow vinyl and download.
Mutiny 2000 Records M2KSA02.

THE MOVIE
(words: Nick Toczek / music: Matt Webster)

Nick Toczek - vocals
Matt Webster - guitars, bass, drums
Simon Nolan - guitar
Keith Jafrate - saxophone
Dee Bo General - vocals

This one began with a bassline that I came up with and wanted to record before I forgot what I was playing, as often happens. I took a drum track initially recorded during a session with Mark on bass and speeded it up a bit to match my new bassline. This done, I added a driving distorted guitar chord riff and a repeating little guitar pattern. I did my usual editing and dropping instruments in and out in the mix, and that was it. I even added a quick spoken vocal and put it out as a Signia Alpha instant classic called, *What Are You Talking To Me For?* in 2019.

I had wanted to put this on *Shooting The Messenger* but we couldn't find a Nick lyric that seemed to fit. I was determined to use this track as the opener for the second album.

I had been in touch with Simon Nolan for the first time in a couple of years and found out he had facilities to record at his home in Sheffield. In the original line-up of Zed, Nogsy was known for his driving guitar style and frequent use of a wah-wah pedal, so I asked him to play something similar. I panned my rhythm guitar to the left and his to the right in the mix. Keith added some great sax soloing and that was the music side done.

After trying a few things, Nick came out with the strange imagery of his *You Write The Book* lyric, which worked well with the music, and the track became *The Movie*. Dee Bo had come to the studio to perform the rap part on the song *Cannibals Of The Western World*. After he'd done that, I thought he might add something interesting to this one, which he did.

BEST WISHES
(words: Nick Toczek / music: Matt Webster & Wulf Ingham)

Nick Toczek - vocals
Matt Webster - guitars, drums, keyboards
Wulf Ingham - guitars, lead guitar
Paul Gray - bass
Keith Jafrate - saxophone
Chris Walsh - flute

I'd gone down to the studio in January 2020 with Nick to record a batch of drum tracks. At that point, I had imagined that the new album would be funk orientated and I wanted the drums to have that kind of feel. Playing the drums on your own, with no accompaniment, can be a very tedious job. I decided to play along to some other songs that had the kind of feel I was looking for. The aim was not to try and play along exactly with a particular track but to play in time and capture the feel of playing with other musicians.

I recorded five or six songs like this, with Michael Jackson and Peter Gabriel tracks playing in my headphones. I did three takes of each drum track; one straightforward, one with a bit more variation and one with lots of fills and stops. I'd seen a documentary of XTC recording their *Nonsuch* album where their session drummer worked this way. The producer then used what he wanted of the drummer's performance in the editing stage.

I sent one of these drum tracks to my old friend and bandmate Wulf Ingham, whom I had not seen for over thirty years. In recent years, we had been in touch on Facebook and nearly got together to record something, with Mark on bass, a couple of years before. This would have been a semi reunion of The Nerve Agents, a band we were all in 1984, but it didn't happen.

Wulf had arranged to come over from Bootle to record at the studio in March 2020. This was delayed, due to the Covid lockdown, until September. I wanted Wulf to appear on this album and add his heavy guitar sound and soloing to a few tracks; luckily, he could do it remotely as he had some home recording facilities.

I sent Wulf what, in my mind, was a funky drum track. As I know he favours loud guitars that play at 11 from start to finish, I asked him to 'leave some gaps'. He interpreted this as a heavy riff that stopped and started and another lead guitar track throughout. I thought this was a good foundation for a track. I added a fairly uninspired bassline before putting the track to one side, feeling it needed something else.

In the summer of 2020, one of my favourite bass players advertised that he was open to remote session work while no gigs were happening in the UK. Paul Gray had recently rejoined The Damned for their *Evil Spirits* album in 2018, having most notably, from my point of view, been their bass player from 1980 to 1983. He had played on T*he Black Album, Friday The Thirteenth EP* and the *Strawberries* album in what I consider to be The Damned's best line-up.

Thinking it would be a dream come true to have Paul Gray play bass on

NICK TOCZEK ᴀᴛ SIGNIA ALPHA

Best Wishes

a track, I looked to find something suitable. The basic version of what later became Best Wishes was there on the reserve pile at this point. In a bid to have a track strong enough to pique his interest, I came up with an intro and middle section, added lots of guitars and keyboards, and rearranged the song to have some interesting stops and starts.

Paul had mentioned in his post that he would only play on projects that resonated with him, so I was glad when he told me he liked it. I sent him the drums and guitars/keyboards via We Transfer, which has proved to be a vital tool for sending audio files back and forth.

A couple of days later, I received an email back saying he had spent a couple of hours trying to put it to a click track. The problem was, although it had started off in time, my editing and swapping bits around had led to the track drifting, time-wise, as I hadn't been working to a click track. Feeling embarrassed that I'd wasted his time, I set to re-editing the backing track to a click track and making sure everything locked into that.

As a result of his advice, I've meticulously locked everything to a click track on every project I've done since. This has made things a lot easier when people add instruments remotely and when I've had to rearrange songs. In a band, you arrange songs as you rehearse them and shorten or lengthen sections as required. The way we write for these albums means that arrangements chop and change after instruments are recorded, often to accommodate the vocals.

Once the timing issues were sorted out, Paul sent back three different, equally good bass tracks and an overdub for the middle section. I compiled these into a master bassline. Both Wulf and I were overjoyed that he had used the same Rickenbacker bass guitar he played on *The Black Album*.

After a pause in the track, just before the main guitar solo comes in, Paul had done a great little bass fill which was only half as long as I needed. To get around this, I reversed the part and added it to the original. When he heard what I'd done, he said he really liked the reversed bass bit.

Once the flute and sax were recorded, there was scope in the mix to highlight different solos and even have duelling guitar/sax/flute solos at the end in a slight nod to The Beatles' three lead guitar duel in *The End* on *Abbey Road*.

With all the other instruments on, the original drums didn't seem to fit anymore, so I recorded new live drums at the studio.

It took a while to find the right lyric for this as it worked so well as an instrumental. Nick's poem *Best Wishes* seemed to fit the bill and was slightly rewritten to work in the context of the music.

Paul Gray liked the finished result and used the song on his website (Paulgrayonline) to promote his remote session work. He also promoted it on his Facebook page, adding, "There's also a rather nifty bit of backwards bass guitar in there somewhere, an art that I admit to not having quite mastered yet in real life..."

CONFIDENCE TRICK

(words: Nick Toczek / music: Matt Webster)

Nick Toczek - vocals
Matt Webster - bass, drums, guitars, mandolin
Wulf Ingham - guitars, lead guitar
Keith Jafrate - saxophone

This one started with the bassline. I wrote that while waiting for the AA to turn up to start my partner Britt's car after the battery had gone flat during the first lockdown of 2020. I had one of my drum tracks ready to go on the computer, so I recorded the bass straight away. I added some sparse guitar parts and the chorus riff which I doubled up with my Ibanez mandolin. I wanted the choruses to contrast with the verses and be loud and heavy, so I asked Wulf to play on the chorus and middle bit. He also added some excellent lead guitar at the end of the song. Keith's saxophone I used sparingly, where I thought it was most effective.

For the Signia Alpha version of this track, singer Paul Tunnicliffe wrote and sang the lyrics. It was released online as a single (with a lyric video) under the title *Starlight*. I had got to know Paul in the mid-1990s after he'd been the vocalist of Bradford death metal pioneers, Slammer. We'd both lived in the same house in 1998 (along with Harris) where we had primitive recording facilities (PZM mics, a cassette four-track and a DAT recorder). We had co-written a couple of tracks that we had roughly recorded but left unfinished. When I set up my home recording equipment in 2018, I thought it would be nice to finish those, with Paul's vocals and lyrics and my music. These two songs were released online as *Mrs Abel* and *Anyway* by Signia Alpha. *Starlight* was our third collaboration.

For our album version, Nick used his poem *Confidence Trick*.

MOON ABOVE THE MÖVENPICK

(words: Nick Toczek / music: Matt Webster)

Nick Toczek - vocals
Matt Webster - drums, acoustic guitars
Mark Cranmer - double bass
Keith Jafrate - saxophone
Chris Walsh - flute

A brushed drum pattern, played on my Premier Royal Ace snare drum, was the starting point for this track, recorded in summer 2018. Up to this point, I had only been recording drum patterns to test my front room recording set-up. I hadn't touched a guitar since about 2003, although my Gordon Smith G2 and my Tanglewood acoustic had been sitting in their cases in the corner of the room.

Struggling to remember a few chords, I miked up my acoustic guitar and recorded a simple chord sequence and a simple melody line. The track was left like this until I thought we needed a jazz-style tune for the new album. Mark added a lovely double bass before Keith and Chris recorded their parts. To say they recorded at different times, without hearing what the other had played, I was amazed how beautifully the saxophone and flute intertwined and worked together. Nick's poem, written in Doha, matched the Eastern feel of the music perfectly.

ALGEBRA

(words: Nick Toczek / music: Matt Webster & Jack Atkinson)

Nick Toczek - vocals
Matt Webster - drums, keyboards
Jack Atkinson - guitar
Mark Cranmer - bass
Keith Jafrate - saxophone
Chris Walsh - flute

This began with live drums and guitar from the February session with Jack. Then Mark sent me his funky bassline, recorded in Cornwall. When lockdown restrictions were lifted in the summer, both Keith and then Chris came to the studio on different days to record their parts.

THE DETECTIVE

(words & music: Matt Webster)

Nick Toczek - vocals
Matt Webster - organ, guitar

In some alternative universe, this was the theme to a massively popular 1960s detective show! In this universe, it was written and recorded by me in 1998 while on a Music Technology course at Bradford College. I found it on an old DAT tape a few years ago and was determined to use it somewhere. I knew what it was about so ended up writing the lyric as well.

CANNIBALS OF THE WESTERN WORLD

(words: Nick Toczek / music: Matt Webster)

Nick Toczek - vocals
Matt Webster - guitars, bass, drums, keyboards
Simon Nolan - guitar
Keith Jafrate - saxophone
Dee Bo General - vocals

This one began with a drum pattern to which I added a bassline and then the guitar riff. Nogsy added his guitar, which I mixed in the right channel and mine in the left. I edited Keith's sax to jump in dramatically after the second chorus. It didn't take long to find the right lyric for this one and we recorded it in a couple of takes. It was an obvious one for Dee Bo to add to, so Nick wrote an additional rap section.

Cannibals Of The Western World was released as a single and also appeared on the cover-mounted *Un Herd 88* CD, given away with the July/August 2020 issue of *RnR Magazine*.

NOTHING RESOLVES

(words: Nick Toczek / music: Matt Webster & Mark Cranmer)

Nick Toczek - vocals
Matt Webster - drums, guitars, keyboards, bongos
Mark Cranmer - bass
Keith Jafrate - saxophone
Chris Walsh - flute
Dee Bo General - vocals

This is one of two backing tracks Mark and I recorded for this album at the studio in January 2020. He had come up from Cornwall, where he was now living, to visit Bradford and see me play in punk/new wave covers band Plastic Letters on the 17th (the last time I played live before lockdown came in). We recorded the bass and drums for this the day after. Nick's poem of frustration (originally entitled *The Usual Poem*) was adapted to this song when we got a chance to record the vocals in August. Dee Bo added his section shortly after.

HOTEL MUSIC

(words: Nick Toczek / music: Matt Webster)

Nick Toczek - vocals
Matt Webster - drums, acoustic guitars
Mark Cranmer - fretless bass
Keith Jafrate - saxophone
Chris Walsh - flute

This one followed the same pattern as *Moon Above The Mövenpick*. It began with another of my drums and acoustic guitar backings, recorded in 2018. Fretless bass this time, from Mark, is counterbalanced by beautiful intertwining sax and flute by Keith and Chris. Nick's eastern hotel tale, also written in Doha, matches the atmosphere.

GALLEON

(words: Nick Toczek / music: Matt Webster & Jack Atkinson)

Nick Toczek - vocals
Matt Webster - drums, bass, mandolin
Jack Atkinson - guitar
Keith Jafrate - saxophone
Chris Walsh - flute
Crazy Bob - purrs

The second track on the album from the session with Jack. After Nick's ghostly tale was recorded I added a mandolin and cut some sections back to just mandolin and flute to try and give that sea shanty feel. Lastly, I added some purrs from a little video clip of my cat Crazy Bob that I had on my iPhone. My small furry pal had moved himself into my house as a kitten in 2006 and refused to leave. He had been my constant companion through good and bad times ever since. Bob had often sat watching me while I recorded and mixed music on my computer. I was heartbroken when he was found dead in a nearby garden at the end of February 2020 after going missing the day before. I thought it fitting that he play the part of ghost cat in a cameo as the track fades out.

CLOSE UP

(words: Nick Toczek / music: Mark Cranmer & Matt Webster)

Nick Toczek - vocals
Matt Webster - drums, acoustic guitar, keyboards
Mark Cranmer - bass
Wulf Ingham - lead guitar
Simon Nolan - acoustic guitar
Keith Jafrate - saxophone
Chris Walsh - flute

This started with Mark's bassline. We initially recorded a faster version with a Motown beat but I thought it might sound better slowed down with a half-paced drum beat.

I had this in mind to be the epic closing track and Wulf took this on board as he recorded magnificent shredding guitar throughout. Keith's sax was next, followed by flute from Chris.

Although this album was recorded during the Covid-19 pandemic, we didn't want it to be a lockdown album or focus too heavily on the situation. However, we did feel that it shouldn't pass without mention, so we chose Nick's emotionally charged *Close Up* poem from his recently published *Corona Diary* book. I then had to mix the song around the dark mood of the poem, which led to the recording of acoustic guitars by both Nogsy and me to add some light and shade to the mix.

THE COLUMBUS MEMOIRS

Produced by Matt Webster.

Recorded and mixed by Matt Webster.

Additional recording by Wulf Ingham, Keith Jafrate, Simon Nolan and Paul Gray.

Recorded 2021, 2018.

Released June 4, 2022, on transparent blue and white vinyl.

Mutiny 2000 Records M2KSA03.

THE HOUR GLASS
(words: Nick Toczek & Matt Webster / music: Matt Webster)

Nick Toczek - vocals
Matt Webster - guitars, drums, keyboards, vocals
Wulf Ingham - guitars, guitar solos
Paul Gray - bass
Keith Jafrate - saxophone
Chris Walsh - flute
Harris - sci-fi strat, vocals

This one began with a keyboard idea. I could hear a cyclic pattern that evoked a feeling of 'time' to me. I managed to pair this with a tom-heavy drum pattern that I had recorded at the studio and worked this up into a full track with just keyboards and drums. I wanted the chorus section to have a loud guitar coming in as a contrast to the intro and verse sections and asked Wulf to remotely record this and also do some lead. In typical Wulf style, he sent me back about three or four different solos; one at the end and a double-tracked solo for the middle section.

I sent this version to Paul Gray, who wasn't sure what to play at first. I asked him to imagine a sci-fi TV adventure theme such as *The Avengers* or, my all-time favourite, John Barry's theme to *The Persuaders*. It turned out that the first thing he learnt to play on keyboards was *The Persuaders* theme tune, so he got where I was coming from, sending me a couple of very different, but both brilliant takes of his bass. I edited these onto the track, in some places using two basslines at once. After this, I rolled back some of the keyboards and added a few new guitar parts. There's a section in the song where everything drops out apart from a tinny keyboard loop. This is supposed to sound like a scratched old record stuck in a groove before the track kicks in again with Wulf's solo.

After the flute and sax parts were done, we had a real problem finding a lyric to fit. I initially recorded a lyric about Willam Shatner's trip into space, called *A Slave To Enterprise* (which I wrote and Harris read), before suggesting that Nick and I exchange lines about time.

I sang the vocals on the chorus with Harris, who also added some 'sci-fi effects' by making strange noises on his Stratocaster.

ANOTHER SHORELINE
(words: Nick Toczek / music: Matt Webster)

Nick Toczek - vocals
Matt Webster - guitars, drums, vocals, ukulele
Paul Gray - Fender bass
Simon Nolan - mandolin, vocals
Harris - vocals

This was the last track written for the album and the quickest to be finished. I came up with the riff on my Fender EOB Stratocaster and recorded it straight away over one of my drum tracks, recorded the year before. Paul Gray liked it and recorded his bassline the next day, although it was a couple of days before it got to me. He had sent it to LA first, by mistake, to someone making a track that also had Mike Garson on keyboards! Also, unusually for Paul Gray, a devotee of the Rickenbacker bass, he played his newly acquired 1964 Fender Precision bass on this one.
Nick had initially recorded the lyrics onto a different backing track. I thought they worked better on this song and swapped them over. I came up with and sang the chorus refrain and then Harris and Nogsy strengthened up my vocal. To finish the track, Nogsy added some high-end mandolin and I played a little riff on the ukulele.

TIME TRIPPER
(words: Nick Toczek / music: Matt Webster)

Nick Toczek - vocals
Matt Webster - acoustic 6 & 12 string guitars, guitars, drums
Paul Gray - bass
Chris Walsh - flute
Keith Jafrate - saxophone
Harris - guitar
Mark Cranmer - keyboards

I wrote the tune for this one on my Fender Joe Strummer Campfire electro-acoustic guitar. I added drums played in my front room on my Premier Signia kit. I wanted the track to go from an acoustic intro to a heavier verse part, so I added a distorted Telecaster rhythm guitar. After this, I played some lead parts on the Telecaster and my 12-string acoustic.

Paul Gray recorded his part using the same Rickenbacker bass guitar he played on The Damned's *Black Album*. For the middle eight, he sent me two separate takes. On one, he told me he couldn't resist playing his bassline from The Damned's *Life Goes On*, a track from their 1982 album, *Strawberries*. He said I could use the other take if I didn't like it. Of course, I used his Damned bassline! That same bassline was copied by both Killing Joke and, more famously, by Nirvana on *Come As You* are from their *Nevermind* album. I suppose he had every right to reclaim it and I was more than happy that he used it on my tune!

When Nick wrote the vocal for this, I asked him to add the phrase 'life goes on' over that section as a nod to the original.

Chris's flute echoes my intro and Keith comes in with some sax breaks as the song builds up. Harris's guitar backs up my electric rhythm parts and adds some incidental lead.

THREADS

(words: Nick Toczek / music: Matt Webster)

Nick Toczek - vocals
Matt Webster - drums, bass, guitars, mandolin
Harris - guitar
Simon Nolan - guitar
Keith Jafrate - saxophone

In August 2020, we were given notice to quit the rehearsal room/ studio we had been renting since 2016, another fallout from the Covid-19 situation. This meant I had three months to try to record everything I needed for this album and anything else I could cram in. This included recording a reunion 7-inch vinyl single with my old band Western Dance, about ten drum tracks for an album Wulf was doing, sessions for Nick's vocals, plus a day each recording Chris and Keith.

Also, during this period, I recorded several more drum tracks in different styles that I could use for the next album. The drums for this track were the last to be recorded in that studio before I had to dismantle my studio kit. That kit consisted of a Premier Black Shadow Resonator 24" kick drum and 16" floor tom, Premier Genista toms a Premier brass 2025 snare drum with Paiste Signature cymbals. It was a real luxury to have that kit permanently set up and miked up into a Tascam 16-channel digital input unit. All I had to do was plug a laptop into that unit and my monitors and headphones and play.

About a year later, I was listening to things I had recorded during that period and rediscovered this drum pattern. I wrote the initial music on the bass and then recorded guitars, adding mandolins in the middle section. I wanted this to be a guitar-heavy song, to which end I asked both Harris and Nogsy (both former Zed guitarists) to play on it. I mixed Keith's sax to come in as a surprise just before the middle-eight, so listen to the track before reading this...

An industrial kind of track needed a lyric to match and Nick came up with the wonderful *Threads*.

DEAD LINES

(words: Nick Toczek / music: Matt Webster)

Nick Toczek - vocals
Matt Webster - keyboards, drums
Mark Cranmer - double bass
Keith Jafrate - saxophone
Emmanuel Williams - guitar
Chris Walsh - flute

Not long into the recording of *Walking The Tightrope*, I became plagued by a serious finger problem. The fingertips on my left hand began continually splitting and peeling, causing great pain when playing stringed instruments. This was probably caused, or made worse, by a nickel allergy. I had changed all my nickel guitar strings for stainless steel ones but the damage was already done. I didn't think I'd be able to play guitars on this new album so I began writing songs on keyboards.

Initially imagined as possible music for a film someone was making about Nick's dad and uncle (see his website for details), I tried to evoke the feel of a post-war New York piano bar. I imagined cigarette smoke and bourbon, broads at the bar, actresses waiting tables. Maybe Lenny Bruce is in for a late-night drink after a show.

Luckily, with my limited skills on the ivories, I was easily able to emulate a sloppy, drunken, late-night piano player. A front room brushed snare and cymbal added to the atmosphere. It then needed some authentic musicianship in the shape of Mark on double bass, Keith on sax, and Chris on flute, all in their element on this track. Emmanuel, who had not appeared on the *Walking The Tightrope* album, made a return to the fold with some lovely lead guitar runs.

JUST FOR A MOMENT

(words & music: Matt Webster)

Chris Walsh - vocals
Matt Webster - Fender telecaster
Mark Cranmer - double bass
Keith Jafrate - saxophone
Emmanuel Williams - lead guitar

The issue with my fingers was causing me real problems but I discovered that wearing a cotton glove meant I could painlessly play the guitar again. As a reward to myself, I bought a new Fender USA Telecaster and began playing guitar every day.

One of the first things I came up with during this new burst of activity was a strange, empty B chord that I liked the sound of so much I wrote a tune around it.

I had also just bought a Fender delay pedal and liked how the first chord echoed into the emptiness. I quickly recorded the song in a couple of takes.

We initially recorded a piece by Nick about a swan for this which I didn't think quite worked. Timings on the album meant I had to shorten the tune anyway, so I needed an alternative lyric.

Mark and Keith had both recorded and sent their parts by the time Chris came to record his flute. He didn't think flute was needed on this so I asked him to try reading the few words I'd written. The lyrics are described elsewhere in this book but they struck a chord with Chris. They brought to mind a dear friend of ours, Adam Bennett (a talented guitarist and singer), who had died in 2014. The song wasn't written about him, but it could have been. The way Chris read the words was very affecting so I wanted to keep his vocal on the finished track.

On the final mix, I cut everything except my Telecaster out until after the vocals had finished.

MOONWATCHERS

(words: Nick Toczek / music: Matt Webster)

Nick Toczek - vocals
Matt Webster - acoustic guitars, guitars, drums, keyboards, vocals
Paul Gray - bass
Wulf Ingham - guitars, guitar solos
Keith Jafrate - saxophone
Chris Walsh - flute
Harris - vocals

This one was another written on my Telecaster. It felt to me like a Gothic type of tune with a slight feel of The Damned's *Dr Jekyll & Mr Hyde* from *The Black Album* about it. I already had it in mind to ask Paul Gray to play on it so I was delighted when he agreed.

Wulf played the heavier guitars in the chorus and some lead at the end. I thickened the sound up with acoustic guitars before Chris and Keith added their parts.

I came up with an intro section a while later. I played this on my 12-string Fender Villager acoustic guitar and edited it onto the beginning of the song.

Nick already had the poem about the moon, which I thought fitted with the Gothic feel, and I asked him to add the bit about the werewolf over the sinister-sounding middle eight.

I felt it needed something else, so I wrote the chorus and sang it with Harris. What would a self-respecting werewolf drink? It could only be absinthe.

I had been introduced to that double-edged sword whilst living in Prague. Harris and I had both indulged in that mystical spirit when our band, Grim, was based in the Czech Republic in 1994. Late one night, on a boat bar on the river Vltava, an incident with a bottle of absinthe, a Russian princess, and some metal tables left me with a broken foot, not the ideal situation for a drummer and the only driver in the band! It spelt the beginning of the end for Grim's sojourn in Prague, but that's another story...

FOUR AND A HALF

(words: Nick Toczek / music: Matt Webster & Jack Atkinson)

Nick Toczek - vocals
Matt Webster - drums, keyboards, guitars, bongos
Jack Atkinson - lead guitar
Mark Cranmer - bass
Simon Nolan - mandolin
Keith Jafrate - saxophone
Chris Walsh - flute

The drums and guitar for this track were from a session with Jack Atkinson in January 2020. I had left this to one side as we had planned to work and develop ideas further but, due to the Covid situation, we didn't get a chance to do that. This song is Jack's only appearance on this album.

As the basic drums and Jack's guitar licks sounded good, I wrote a verse around that using a Stevie Wonder-type clavinet keyboard sound. I came up with a new chorus section which felt to me like something from the theme from *The Godfather*, then added guitars on the chorus section and the verses.

Mark played some slap bass which I ended up cutting up and looping. Nogsy then added a couple of mandolins to the mix, followed by Keith's sax and Chris's flute.

Nick's tale of stupidity and gun threat seemed to fit with the gangster feel I had aimed for in the music.

When we began looking at the lyrics for this album, we did two socially distanced vocal recording sessions in a large room at Keighley Creative. At the second of these sessions, a TV crew, there to get comments on Bradford's bid to be UK City of Culture in 2025, filmed us recording some vocals and interviewed Nick. A brief section of this was shown that evening on *Calendar*, ITV's local news programme, with all mention of our album carefully edited out!

THE COLUMBUS MEMOIRS

(words: Nick Toczek / music: Mark Cranmer, Keith Jafrate & Matt Webster)

Nick Toczek - vocals
Matt Webster - drums, bongos
Mark Cranmer - double bass
Keith Jafrate - saxophone
Simon Nolan - guitars
Chris Walsh - flute
Wulf Ingham - lead guitar

This was one of the first tracks Nick and I worked on for the whole project. The initial track consisted of my drums, Mark on double bass, Keith on sax and Emmanuel Williams on guitar. When The Moon reconvened for a jam session in the autumn of 2018, it was the first time they had played together in over thirty years. I used my new drum mics while Mark set up and recorded the session. This was the first of about seven long jams we did that day. I listened through and did rough mixes of a few of those jams with a mind to use them for the project with Nick. Unfortunately, Emmanuel's guitar wasn't recorded well and was unusable, so I did an initial mix with just the bass, sax and drums.

Nick and I had our first recording session in Autumn 2019. He had brought a file of poems and stories that we were going through. This one immediately stood out. Having recorded it, we felt it was too long to use on the first LP, so it was shelved. When we started working on the third album, I wanted to use it. I thought a way to include such a long track was to use it as the heart of the album. We named the album after the track and referenced some of the themes raised in the lyric in other songs.

In the end, it was cut from nearly ten minutes down to a more manageable length. Nogsy was keen to be on this and worked out a rhythm guitar part and some lead. Chris added flute, and I played bongos and percussion. I thought it would be nice to bring in a different flavour later in the track, so Wulf added some wild Zappa style distorted lead guitar. Definitely one of my favourite Nick lyrics.

DIGNITY

(words: Nick Toczek / music: Matt Webster & Wulf Ingham)

Nick Toczek - vocals
Matt Webster - drums, bass,12 string acoustic guitar, vocals
Wulf Ingham - guitars, lead guitar, slide guitar, mandolin, harmonica
Keith Jafrate - saxophone
Chris Walsh - flute, vocals
Harris - guitar, vocals

I recorded the drum track for this one for another project and wanted to build a new track around it. At the second studio recording session I had with Wulf in September 2020, I asked him to play something to go with it. He came up with this great bluesy riff that I mixed and edited and added a bassline before sending it back to him. He decided to re-record his rhythm guitars and added lead guitar, not one but three solos at the end, and bits of mandolin and mouth organ. I played my Fender Villager 12-string acoustic guitar to contrast Wulf's heavy guitars, which I could then drop in and out. The intro is my 12-string riff reversed.

This was another of Nick's vocals recorded at Keighley Creative. I re-edited the arrangement to better suit the vocals and added the 'just give me some dignity' backing vocal, which Chris doubled after he played his flute part. This vocal was added to and improvised on by Harris, who also added extra guitar. Keith's sax was the finishing touch.

This was now a powerful emotional and musical track and was always planned as the album's closing track. We also decided on this as the first single.

PART 3: THE PLAYERS

A FEW MORE SANDS FROM THE HOUR GLASS

By Matt Webster

N early all the musicians appearing on our three albums to date are friends with whom I have played music in the past. The exceptions are Dee Bo General, a friend of Nick's, and Paul Gray, one of my all-time favourite bass guitarists from one of my favourite bands, The Damned.

One of the high points for me in doing these albums has been the chance to play (even if remotely) with old friends and new ones, all of whom have generously contributed performances and ideas and added enormously to the whole project.

I'll attempt to introduce them to you in the order I originally got to know them through a series of overlapping threads that stemmed from the Bradford punk scene of the early eighties.

MARK CRANMER

Mark and I started our musical journey together, although we have only played together for about three years out of the last forty. In 1980 we decided to form a band with some friends (including my cousin Jane, whom Mark later married). My brother Nick had two guitars, an electric and an acoustic, which I attempted to learn to play using Bert Weadon's *Learn To Play In A Day* book. Having just about mastered *Ghost Riders In The Sky* and at least three chords, I began to struggle with the tuning further up the neck, not realising at the time that both guitars had bent necks. This meant that they were impossible to tune properly and therefore sounded pretty lousy – not that that stopped me writing

101

most of the songs for my hardcore punk band The Convulsions on them a couple of years later, although I never went past the filth fret!

To add to the untuneable guitars, Mark got a Bontempi keyboard for Christmas 1980. He promptly learned how to play Jona Lewie's *Stop The Cavalry*, which was in the charts at the time, and later, *Thrown Away* by The Stranglers. By this time, I'd decided I wanted to play the drums and had bought a snare drum (with no snare wires) from a lad at school and a cheap Zyn cymbal and stand.

I had started to put by money from my weekly paper round delivering *The Shipley Target* (a weekly free sheet paper I would end up working on and writing music reviews for years later). I also saved my school dinner

money and bus fare (living off crisps and Marathon bars for school dinner for the next year). Mark informed me that his school was selling a drum kit. With what I'd saved and a bit more, I managed to buy it. Much to the delight of my parents and neighbours, I began practising in the front room, playing along to early albums by The Stranglers, The Clash, The Damned, The Jam, SLF, Blondie and Elvis Costello.

Every Wednesday, Mark's dad, Dennis, would pick up my yellow 1960s Premier Olympic drum kit and our one amp and guitar in his Robin Reliant. With the car full, Mark and I were left to walk to the local youth club, the Springfield in Thorpe Edge, where we would set up our gear and mess about with other young punk rockers trying to play songs like *Clash City Rockers* or *God Save The Queen* without knowing any of the chords.

In 1981, with Mark now on my brother's rubbish guitar, me on drums, and our friend Russell Spence on bass, we formed our punk band, The Hate. Richard 'Pee Wee' Priestly, the fourth member, lived opposite me. A few months before, Richard's dad, Mike, who wrote and reviewed albums for local newspaper *The Telegraph & Argus* (a paper I later worked for), had given him a review copy of the new LP by The Damned. This was *The Black Album*, which we both sat and listened to weeks before it was released. I loved the album instantly; the collection of great songs with little acoustic linking pieces was musically stunning. The sound of The

Damned had changed on this album, partly due to the introduction of a new bass player, Paul Gray, formerly of Eddie & the Hot Rods.

After a few days, I convinced Richard to sell me the album as he wasn't that bothered about it. The only problem was I had no money spare. My solution was to get my eldest brother, Martin, to buy it. I was lucky in having two older brothers who both had extensive record collections that I could listen to and make tapes from, including loads of early punk and new wave stuff. A short while later, *The Black Album* found its way into my album box, where it stayed. One afternoon in the summer holidays, The Hate set up to rehearse in Richard's front room. After a while, we noticed a crowd of young girls watching up through the window. Having exhausted our three-song repertoire, we plugged a tape player through our amplifier and gave a great show to those on the street by miming to Stiff Little Fingers' *Hanx!* album.

In 1982, a one-off rehearsal/recording with a band called The Desire Crew led to our first gig together. Mark was on a course at the Cathedral Centre, which ran YOP training courses for the young unemployed. The canteen there was turned into a stage as The Desire Crew supported Christian rock band Autumn Gold.

After The Desire Crew disintegrated, Mark and I ended up in different bands with former school friends. He was in Raw, and I was in The Convulsions with Kenny Armitage, Phil Hey and Tony 'Stan' Flaherty. Both bands played whenever we could on the Bradford punk scene, alongside bands like The Negativz, Anti System, Requiem, Isolation, Subvert and Chronic.

The Desire Crew folded into a band called the Vegetable Section that I was in initially but dropped out. Mark continued with guitarist Paul Arron and others (including Nogsy on drums for a while) for the next couple of years.

In 1984, Mark and Raw singer Liam Sheeran (fresh from a spell as the

103

singer for Anti System, replacing Nogsy) decided they wanted a more musical band. They linked up with guitarist Pete Ingham (later Wulf) and local ranting poet Mike 'Dirk Spig' Hughes on piano (these bloody poets get everywhere!). I was asked to join on drums, and we became The Nerve Agents.

After recording a demo of seven tracks (recorded at Lion Studios) and half a dozen gigs, Mark decided to leave and continue with guitarist Paul Arron in the Vegetable Section.

Mark later joined saxophonist Keith Jafrate and Emmanuel Williams's jazz band The Moon. I was asked to stand in on drums for their first two performances as a four-piece, at Manningham Community Centre, in 1985. Mark also played bass for my next band, Western Dance, in 1986 and played on the B side of our first single.

The next time Mark and I played together was with blues guitarist Roger Higgins' Bottleneck Boogie Band in 1990. Mark was the regular bass player; I stood in on drums for a couple of gigs until joining full time... just as Mark left! I played with that band on and off until 2004.

Mark played in bands Otis & The Elevators and Hot Spiced Bananas until 1993 before hanging up his bass for seventeen years. He returned to play in punk covers band Snuff Rock in 2010. Over the next few years, he amassed a lot of instruments and other music gear and set up recording facilities in his shared rehearsal rooms.

In early 2016, as well as playing in punk band Mammoth Tank, Mark joined The Johnny Gray Band. The group, who played rock and blues covers, featured two guitarists, Jack Atkinson (who later played on all three Nick Toczek & Signia Alpha albums) and Dave Myatt. I joined in December 2016. A few months later, we set about recording some rehearsals for promo purposes.

When singer Johnny Gray departed, the band was renamed Lenin Black and, for the first half of 2018, also featured Harris on vocals. Mark moved to live in Cornwall in January 2019, where he joined tribute band Slide Oasis.

SIMON NOLAN 'NOGSY'

Simon and I were born three days apart in March 1966 and were probably in the same maternity ward at St Luke's Hospital, Bradford.

I first met Simon, or 'Nogsy' as he introduced himself, in September 1982 at a place called the Cathedral Centre, which was running vari-ous government train-ing schemes under the banner of the Youth Opportunities Programme (YOP). We both started at the same time, he was on the printing course whilst I was on the 'Radio Team'.

The Cathedral Centre was a hive of activity in those days, attracting a mass of creative punk kids to a place that paid £25 a week (much better than signing on in those days) for a year to learn how to screenprint, edit tape or, if you preferred, office, woodworking or building skills. This was a golden opportunity for us young punks to print posters, flyers and t-shirts for our bands and try to scrounge a bit of recording time. Mark was already there, having started in January on the Radio Team.

My second 'recording session' took place at the Cathedral Centre. The 'studio' there was equipped with former BBC reel-to-reel tape machines usually used for recording and editing a talking magazine for the blind. The session began with capturing the first-ever noise commit-ted to tape by The Convulsions, followed by a one-song effort from an untested line-up. I played the drums, Nogsy played guitar, and Mark Cranmer sang and played bass to the Webster/Cranmer composition *Hassled Youth*. This one song was then performed live (with the addi-tion of Mickey Knowles) by us as The Hassled in between slots by main and support bands at about half a dozen local punk gigs. This song was also in the sets of both The Convulsions and Mark's band Raw. Hardly a classic, but songs were hard to come by in those days!

One day, Nogsy turned up with a demo tape from a band he'd just joined, called Anti-System, for which he was now the singer. This tape was far superior to the recorded output from any of our fledgling bands thus far, having been recorded in the 8-track Lion Studios in Leeds, which became the studio of choice for the next few years. Nogsy sang on Anti-System's *Defence Of The Realm EP* and tracks on two Pax Records punk compilation albums. He left Anti-System in 1984 and formed punk band Morbid Humour, releasing the single *Oh, My God*.

In 1986, he and I briefly joined forces in a short-lived band called God, which never got past the rehearsal stage. Our biggest claim to fame was that the studio owner where we practised (Flexible Response) refused to let us book rehearsals under our name and insisted on calling us Blasphemy.

By 1989, Nogsy was the guitarist in Bradford rock/post-punk band Zed (a band I was later a member of) who released the 12-inch vinyl EP *Easy Does It* and toured around Europe a few times.

After leaving Zed, he was in various other bands in Bradford and Sheffield, including Slack (with Harris), Moota, The Boneyard Boys, UkeWind, SpyBand and The Hazel Leigh Band.

I was pleased to find out he had some home recording gear and could contribute remotely to our albums from his home in Sheffield.

NICK: *In December 1979, I and my then-partner, Kay Russell, produced the first issue of Bradford music zine, The Wool City Rocker. Kay and I then split up, and I went on to publish a further thirteen editions over the next eighteen months, before running out of money. Thereafter, the magazine became a fading memory… until, about twenty years later, when I was contacted, out-of-the-blue, by a guy called Nogsy. He directed me to the 'We're From Bradford' website he'd created which featured details of Bradford fanzines, starting with the covers of every issue of The Wool City Rocker, along with background information and a list of what each edition contained. Now he's also playing on some of these tracks. I owe you big time, Nogsy!*

WULF INGHAM

When I met up with Wulf in the summer of 2020 to record tracks for the Nick Toczek & Signia Alpha albums, it was the first time I'd seen him in over thirty years.

After both Mark and singer Liam Sheeran left The Nerve Agents, Wulf and I joined forces with Dave Wilcox and Rik 'Pox' Leith of the recently disbanded The Negativz and formed Swamp Flower in Autumn 1984. In December, Dave Wilcox left and was replaced by singer Wendy Jepson for an already booked recording session (Lion again). Keyboard player John Jankovich joined shortly after.

That line-up of Swamp Flower lasted for the next twelve months. When Swamp Flower ended, I went on to be in Western Dance, and Wulf reunited with Negatives/Negativz frontman Dave Wilcox in Six Feet Under.

After that band folded, Wulf left Bradford and had numerous adventures, including working at an owl sanctuary. He, too, had a long break from playing. By the time I reconnected with him on Facebook, Wulf had started playing again and was involved in the recording band Wall Of Sound with Negativz/Six Feet Under drummer Tony Fox. He played live in bands including Buzzard, The Vindaloo Experience, Project Zero and most recently, Cumbrian Motorhead tribute band Motorbeard.

Wulf has home recording gear and was able to contribute remotely to *Walking The Tightrope* and *The Columbus Memoirs*. He also co-wrote the music for *Best Wishes* and *Dignity*.

KEITH JAFRATE

I first met Keith in 1985 when I was asked to stand in on drums for The Moon at their first performance as a four-piece at Manningham Community Centre. Over the next year, my band Swamp Flower and The Moon

played around the same venues in Bradford and even joined forces for one gig as Moonflower.

After Emmanuel left The Moon, Keith and Mark continued as The Edge, a three-piece with a new drummer.

Keith spent the nineties leading jazz-poetry trio Sang and went on to start text-music experimentalists Orfeo 5 in 2002. He is currently the leader of jazz quintet Urboro and playing with a variety of other groups. He's also the lyricist for folk collective Army of Briars. Obviously, Keith is no stranger to the concept of mixing poetry with music.

The Moon reunion session in 2018 was the first time I'd seen Keith since the late 1980s. Mark had been in touch with him and done some recording the year before.

NICK: *When Matt told me that he'd asked a brilliant saxophonist called Keith Jafrate to play on some of our album tracks, I was taken aback. I'd forgotten that he was a musician. I'd long ago known him as an accomplished poet. Back in the late 1970s, I'd met the late Bradford poet and publisher, David Tipton, when he invited me to a party at which we both got very drunk and ended up in a fight because he'd*

108

hated me calling my poetry readings 'gigs'. David and I became firm friends and collaborators. He ran Rivelin Press from his Bradford home, publishing mostly poetry books, and sending me copies of everything he published. One of the early ones was 'Finding Space', a 32-page pamphlet that was Keith's first collection. I still have that truly impressive slim volume. Over the next twenty years, through various publishers, Keith authored half a dozen more books and pamphlets, all excellent. To have now re-encounter him as an equally astonishing saxophonist has been wonderful. What an amazing man he is!

EMMANUEL WILLIAMS

When I met Emmanuel through his involvement with the Moon, he lived not far from me, in Shipley. He had recently been a member of the Bradford band 20th Century Hats. Before that, he had been in Birmingham-based studio band Lazy Banana. He also had a studio-based experimental project, Sam Sara & The Delusions (1979-1999), an outlet for his improvisations which featured numerous guest artists.

In late 1986, Emmanuel left The Moon and joined Bradford-based Banghra band Shaan, the backing band for the famous Pakistani movie star and singer Irene Parveen on her UK tour.

The next time I heard about him was over thirty years later when he and Mark arranged The Moon jam session. Emmanuel was now living in Birmingham and had been involved in many musical projects over the years. He is a member of Midlands-based Amen Ra (1993 - present), whose album *Summer Collection* (1994) featured Gambia's leading classical singer Mame Tamsir Njai and was a big radio hit in the Gambia. He has also been involved in Shamanka (1994-1997), a sister band to Amen Ra, and Manu Pedze (1994-present), a mix of African music with European folk and classical undertones, which is essentially a collaboration with Paul Morgan (ex Burning Spear).

STEPHEN ANDREWS

I first met Steve in late 1985 when I bumped into former Nerve Agents singer Liam Sheeran on a bus. He told me about a new band he was getting together with a young guitarist called Stephen Andrews. They were already rehearsing with former Anti-System bassist Mickey Knowles on drums, so I joined as the bass player. The band became Western Dance. We played our first gig at a Red Wedge all-day gig in January 1986, warming up for The Communards, Billy Bragg and The Style Council.

I swapped to drums in time to record a demo EP, *Give Me The Moonlight*. Mark joined on bass shortly after but had left by December, replaced by Ade Clark.

After many gigs and recordings, Western Dance called it a day in the summer of 1989. A band with me on drums, Stephen on guitar and Mark on bass didn't make it past rehearsal stages. Stephen and I reunited with Liam Sheeran in Primate (1990-1995) and Kwai Chang Caine (2001-2007). Stephen was also a member of Zed (1996-1997).

In November 2016, Western Dance reunited to play a one-off thirtieth-anniversary gig, which led to me picking up my drumsticks again.

In 2020, we got together in the studio to record the lockdown single, *In The Distance / This Is Your*, released on vinyl by Mutiny 2000 Records.

I teamed up with Steve again in a new line-up of punk/new wave

covers band Plastic Letters, whom I joined in 2017. Steve had formed the band with singer Peter 'Skinny' Finan, Ade Clark and original Zed drummer Jez Farrar in 2011, and they'd split in 2015. Bassist Jonny Botterell joined the band at the same time as I did.

If you're still reading, things are about to get even more complicated as people weave in and out of each other's bands. By now, it must be evident that the tangled web of the Bradford music scene of the eighties is filtered down into these Signia Alpha recordings.

HARRIS

In the mid-1980s, both Harris and Chris Walsh were members of a band called Handful of Dance. They were on the same circuit as Western Dance and appeared on the same bill a couple of times. I knew their drummer, Jez, who went on to be in Zed. He'd been in a band called JJ's Bones which featured Tiny Munroe singer NJ Wilow.

In 1990, Harris bought a Marshall amp from Stephen so he could make some loud noise when he took over from Nogsy as Zed's guitarist. With Zed, Harris recorded *The Articles Of Captain Mission* album and toured Europe.

I got to know Harris in 1993 when four-fifths of Handful Of Dance had got together in a new band called Nowt. Nowt were more acoustic orientated and featured a lot of harmony vocals, acoustic guitars, mandolin and flute alongside drums, bass and electric guitar. Their songs were delivered with humour and sung in a Bradford accent, mainly by Harris and guitarist and singer Adam Bennett. I joined as the drummer when Jez left in Autumn 1993.

Being disillusioned by the lack of places to play and, to some degree, life in general, Harris, Adam and I resolved to relocate to the Czech Republic. We joined up with former Zed bassist and singer Jont, who had decided to stay in Prague after a tour with The Psycho Surgeons. We planned to live in Prague and play around Europe. Although named on the posters, we arrived in Prague a week late and missed a support to Joe Strummer at the Repre Rock Club, a venue that was to become our base of operations.

Playing under the name of both Nowt (smaller clubs) and Zed (bigger gigs), we had many adventures before an enforced return to the UK that was partly due to Absinthe – but that's another story.

Back in the UK in 1995, we became known as Grim. The band had

111

written a new set and played gigs in Bradford, London and Amsterdam when Harris decided to leave and team up with Nogsy, Jez and former Nowt bassist Boz in the new band Slack. Meanwhile, Jont and I carried on with a new line-up of Zed, which featured guitarists Crispian Baker and, initially, Stephen Andrews. Later, Adam Bennett became our second guitarist when available, as he had moved to Bristol.

I shared a rented house with Harris (and others) from 1997 to 2000, during which time he was also involved in setting up the Mutiny 2000 Studio. We also played together in the last incarnation of The Psycho Surgeons with Jont, Wild Willi Beckett and sax player John Gray. That line-up became known as The Psurgeons and released the single *Kingdom Come, Bring It On!* after the death of frontman Wild Willi Beckett. As a tribute, Willi's ashes were pressed into the lime green vinyl of the seven-inch single.

For the first half of 2018, Harris and I played together in covers band Lenin Black with guitarist Dave Myatt and Mark Cranmer on bass.

Harris has also been involved in numerous other projects and bands, including Shiny Beast, Moota, Owt, Siren, The Richard Harris Experience, Chaing, and as a solo singer-songwriter.

CHRIS WALSH

Chris had brought his flute-playing skills and backing vocals to both Handful of Dance and Nowt, which is when I got to know him. Particularly in Nowt, I thought his flute playing transformed the sound and feel of

Harris and Chris with Adam Bennett RIP. Photo: Richard Ingham RIP.

the songs and was an instrument I had not heard used very much in rock music, Jethro Tull apart. In 1993, I was also listening to Paul Weller's *Wild Wood* album, which featured flute on several tracks.

I had been in touch with Chris on Facebook over the previous few years but had only seen him a couple of times since the late 1980s. When I started making the music for these albums, I immediately wanted to include him.

He came over to record for the first album and ended up on more tracks than expected. He was, of course, invited back for the subsequent two albums.

JACK ATKINSON

I met Jack when we were in The Johnny Gray Band together. He left six months after I joined due to his work commitments as a chef.

He had told me that he was interested in recording some original material and got in touch in 2019 to ask me to record and play drums on a song of his.

From those sessions, we came up with several interesting fragments. I worked three of these into tracks on the *Shooting The Messenger* CD. We had intended to work more together in 2020 but managed one recording session in February before lockdown.

JONNY BOTTERELL

I I first met Jonny when he joined Plastic Letters at the same time as I did. He was a schoolmate of Stephen's and knew many people that I know, but I don't think I'd ever met him in the old days. At this point, he was living in York and playing bass and singing in his other band, Jonny & The Rizlas.

I had set up to record a Plastic Letters rehearsal for promos and also to record a few of Steve's songs on which Jonny played bass. This led to us jamming and recording what became *This City Eats*.

I had intended for Steve and Jonny to record more music for the other albums, but that wasn't possible due to the Covid situation.

DEE BO GENERAL

I hadn't met Dee Bo until he came to record his vocals on *When We Men Talk*. We liked his contribution and invited him back for three tracks on our second album, *Walking The Tightrope*. It was only due to Covid restrictions and bad timing that he didn't appear on *The Columbus Memoirs*.

NICK: *Dee Bo General: In 2005, I did several gigs with three poets from Huddersfield - Bongo Chilli, DanMan, and Dee Bo General. All three were also rappers who performed and recorded with musicians. Dee Bo and I went on to gig together intermittently over the years.*

I introduced him to Authors Abroad who started booking him into schools under the name Donavan Christopher (aka Rapperman). Their imprint, Caboodle Books, published two

114

collections of his poetry for pupils. In return, he introduced me to his Brad-
ford-based musical sidekick, Rootsman who, under his real name, John
Bolloten, is an outstanding professional photographer. His photo session
with me produced the pic that's on the homepage of my website. Dee Bo
and I remain good friends and I was delighted when he agreed to contrib-
ute to some of these album tracks.

PAUL GRAY

Paul Gray joined Eddie & The Hot Rods in 1976. One of his first gigs was at the Marquee Club, where the Hot Rods were supported by the Sex Pistols on their first London appearance.

Paul played on the first three Hot Rods albums, including *Teenage*

Depression, and their 1977 hit single *Do Anything You Wanna Do* before leaving in early 1980. He joined The Damned and played on their next two LPs, *The Black Album* and *Strawber-ries,* their acclaimed *Friday The Thirteenth EP,* and singles including *White Rabbit, (There Ain't No) Sanity Claus* and *Lovely Money.*

I saw Paul play live with The Damned at the *Christmas On Earth* all-day festival at Leeds Queen's Hall in December 1981, a gig Nick Toczek co-organised. Paul's first spell in The Damned was a huge influence on me, Mark, Wulf and a lot of my other musician friends. His bass lines were the subject of much discussion and a rite of passage if you could manage to play one.

After The Damned, Paul joined UFO and went on to play with lots of people (including Wham's Andrew Ridgeley). He also periodically rejoined The Damned and Eddie & The Hot Rods for various projects.

In 2013 he reunited with Captain Sensible in The Sensible Gray Cells before rejoining The Damned full time in 2017. He also plays with former Damned drummer Rat Scabies in Professor & The Madman.

Paul played on the track *Best Wishes* from our second album and four tracks on *The Columbus Memoirs.* He has already recorded bass on a few more tracks for a future Signia Alpha project.

ABOUT NICK TOCZEK

Nick Toczek is a British writer and performer who lives in his hometown of Bradford in Yorkshire. He's published more than fifty books, released numerous albums (of music and of spoken word) and has visited dozens of countries as a writer in schools. He's also a professional magician, puppeteer, radio presenter and music journalist.

Photo by John Bolloten

RECENT PUBLICATIONS

Corona Diary (Mutiny 2000 Publications, 2020) - book of poetry.

Voices In My Head (Caboodle Books, 2020) - book of poetry.

Dragons Are Back! (Caboodle Books, 2016) - book of dragon poems for children.

Haters, Baiters And Would-Be Dictators (Routledge, 2016) - book on the history of anti-Semitism.

Cats'n'Bats'n'Slugs'n'Bugs (Caboodle Books, 2009) - book of children's poems about creatures.

Number, Number, Cut A Cucumber (Caboodle Books, 2009) - book of poems for younger children.

Me And My Poems (Caboodle Books, 2008) - poems for children.

ALBUM RELEASES

Nick Toczek has also collaborated on a number of releases of his poetry and lyrics with musical backing, including:

Nick Toczek & Signia Alpha

Shooting The Messenger (Mutiny 2000 Records, 2020) on vinyl LP, CD & download.

> *'The laid-back, funky, jazz rock vibe that characterises most of this album complements Toczek's distinctive and, as ever, reassuringly calm, but equally commanding Yorkshire burr perfectly.'*
>
> Vive Le Rock!   (Mar/Apr 2020)

Nick Toczek & Thies Marsen

The Bavariations Album (Not-A-Rioty Records, 2019) - on CD & download.

Death And Other Destinations: The Second Bavariations Album (Not-A-Rioty Records, 2021) - on vinyl LP & download.

> *'Setting poems against music is hazardous. Nick Toczek is, thankfully, the kind of poet whose lifestyle and experience aptly suit him to the process. … His counterpart is, suitably, a Bavarian punk and indie musician who … has produced this stunning, innovative album.'*
>
> RnR Magazine (2019)

All the above are available via Nick's website (see below).

CONTACT DETAILS, WEBSITES & INFO.

Nick's website: www.nicktoczek.com

Schools bookings via: www.authorsabroad.com

Wikipedia pages: en.wikipedia.org/wiki/Nick_Toczek

Nick's email: nick.toczek@gmail.com

ABOUT MATT WEBSTER

Matt Webster is a British musician (well, a drummer who manages to get by on a few stringed things) and producer who lives in his hometown of Bradford in Yorkshire. He's published at least two books (on music) and released numerous albums and singles with various bands. He's a former radio presenter and music reviewer who obviously really likes music.

Photo by Britt Jagger

SELECTED MUSICOGRAPHY

The Convulsions - Electro Convulsive Therapy, EP, 1983
Electro Convulsive Therapy, album (re-release compilation), 2001
The Nerve Agents - To And Fro, EP, 1984
Swamp Flower - Shackles On The Mind, single, 1985
Western Dance - Give Me The Moonlight, EP, 1986
What Does It Take?, single, 1987
This Perfect Day, EP, 1987
Live - album, 1987
Western Dance - album (re-release compilation), 2000
30 - album (re-release compilation), 2016
In The Distance / This Is Your... - single 2020
Primate - One Mile From Anywhere, EP, 1990
Feel, EP, 1991
Liquid, EP, 1993
Evolution, album, 1993
Mad Monkey, album (re-release compilation), 2001
Grim - Let It Be Grim, album, 1995, 2000
Zed - Mutiny 2000, album, 1997
Kwai Chang Caine - The Ones That Never Learn, album, 2002
Reel To Real Life, album, 2004
The Psurgeons - Kingdom Come, Bring It On!, single, 2007

Also available from Mutiny 2000 Publications

Bradford's Noise Of The Valleys
by Gary Cavanagh and Matt Webster

Bradford's Noise Of The Valleys is a series of books and CDs that tell the story of the music scene of Bradford and the surrounding areas, including Keighley and Halifax, from the 1960s onwards. Volume One covers the years 1967 to 1987, Volume 2 continues the history between 1988 and 1998.

The books contain hundreds of 'rock family trees' and feature individual profiles of bands and artists and many local clubs and venues. The pages are packed with contemorary photos, articles, posters and images. These cover a massive range of musical styles from pop and rock to folk and blues to indie and punk to hardcore and doom metal to the dance scene.

Also available to compliment the books is a range of CDs showcasing many of the featured bands, including; Tasmin Archer, Terrorvision, New Model Army, Kiki Dee, Paradise Lost, 1919, Verity, The Accent, Smokie, Zed, Slammer, Skeletal Family, Psycho Surgeons, The Invaders, The Negatives, Embrace, Western Dance, Pianoman and Nick Toczek.

'...this work of breathtaking scholarship. Books like this send you spiralling back through the landscapes of your memory...' Ian Clayton

bradfordnoise.com

Lightning Source UK Ltd.
Milton Keynes UK
UKHW020655290322
400773UK00009B/719